CYCLING THE REIVERS ROUTE

CYCLING THE REIVERS ROUTE

COAST TO COAST THROUGH WILD NORTHUMBERLAND'S BORDER COUNTRY

by Rachel Crolla and Carl McKeating

JUNIPER HOUSE, MURLEY MOSS,
OXENHOLME ROAD, KENDAL, CUMBRIA LA9 7RL
www.cicerone.co.uk

© Rachel Crolla and Carl McKeating 2021
First edition 2021
ISBN: 978 1 85284 910 8

Printed in Singapore by KHL Printing on responsibly sourced paper
A catalogue record for this book is available from the British Library.
All photographs are by the author unless otherwise stated.

Route mapping by Lovell Johns www.lovelljohns.com
© Crown copyright 2021 OS PU100012932.
NASA relief data courtesy of ESRI

Updates to this guide

While every effort is made by our authors to ensure the accuracy of guidebooks as they go to print, changes can occur during the lifetime of an edition. This guidebook was researched and written before the COVID-19 pandemic. While we are not aware of any significant changes to routes or facilities at the time of printing, it is likely that the situation will give rise to more changes than would usually be expected. Any updates that we know of for this guide will be on the Cicerone website (www.cicerone.co.uk/910/updates), so please check before planning your trip. We also advise that you check information about such things as transport, accommodation and shops locally. Even rights of way can be altered over time.

We are always grateful for information about any discrepancies between a guidebook and the facts on the ground, sent by email to updates@cicerone.co.uk or by post to Cicerone, Juniper House, Murley Moss, Oxenholme Road, Kendal, LA9 7RL.

Register your book: To sign up to receive free updates, special offers and GPX files where available, register your book at www.cicerone.co.uk.

Front cover: Hawthorn blossom on the climb from Bewcastle (Day 2)

CONTENTS

Map key 7
Route summary tables 8

INTRODUCTION 11
Why choose the Reivers Route? 12
Who were the Reivers? 13
How tough is the ride? 15
How many days? 16
West to east or east to west? 17
Alternative: The Borderers Ride 17
Getting there and back 18
Where to stay 20
What kind of bike? 21
Equipment 22
Carrying your gear 23
What to wear 23
Maps and apps 24
Signage 25
Using this guide 26

THE REIVERS ROUTE: THE FOUR-DAY RIDE 27
Day 1   Whitehaven to Carlisle 30
Day 2   Carlisle to Bailey Mill 47
Day 3   Bailey Mill to Bellingham 57
Day 4   Bellingham to Tynemouth 74

The Borderers Ride: Gretna to Berwick-upon-Tweed 91

Appendix A   Accommodation 118
Appendix B   Bike shops and other useful contacts 123
Appendix C   Further reading 125

Acknowledgements

The authors would like to thank the staff at Bailey Mill for their continued support of Reivers cyclists (and for rustling up a superb afternoon meal during a hard cycling day into headwinds). Thanks to Glen Thistlethwaite and Chris Truss for braving the dark interior of Kielder Forest during prime midge conditions. Thanks also to Harriet Truss, Romily Thistlethwaite, Oli Burns and James Brown. As ever, thanks to our two daughters for their continued enthusiasm and patience throughout the project.

Note on mapping

The route maps in this guide are derived from publicly available data, databases and crowd-sourced data. As such they have not been through the detailed checking procedures that would generally be applied to a published map from an official mapping agency. However, we have reviewed them closely in the light of local knowledge as part of the preparation of this guide.

The grassy road to Colt Crag Reservoir (Day 4)

MAP KEY

Symbols used on route maps

SCALE: 1:100,000

Contour lines are drawn at 50m intervals and labelled at 100m intervals. Route maps are drawn at 1:100,000 (1cm = 1km)

GPX files for all routes can be downloaded free at www.cicerone.co.uk/910/GPX.

Features on the overview map

- County/Unitary boundary
- National boundary
- Urban area
- National Park eg **THE LAKE DISTRICT**
- Area of Outstanding Natural Beauty eg *Solway Coast*

ROUTE SUMMARY TABLES

Reivers Route: Four-day itinerary					
	Start	Finish	Distance	Ascent	Page
Day 1	Whitehaven (NX 969 182)	Carlisle (NY 398 565)	51 miles (82km)	1076m	30
Day 2	Carlisle (NY 398 565)	Bailey Mill (NY 517 785)	34 miles (55km)	683m	47
Day 3	Bailey Mill (NY 517 785)	Bellingham (TQ 374 717)	37 miles (60km)	875m	57
Day 4	Bellingham (TQ 374 717)	Tynemouth (NZ 374 691)	51 miles (82km)	764m	74

Reivers Route: East to west four-day itinerary					
	Start	Finish	Distance	Ascent	Page
Day 1	Tynemouth (NZ 374 691)	Bellingham (TQ 374 717)	51 miles (82km)	859m	90
Day 2	Bellingham (TQ 374 717)	Bailey Mill (NY 517 785)	37 miles (60km)	875m	73
Day 3	Bailey Mill (NY 517 785)	Carlisle (NY 398 565)	34 miles (55km)	598m	56
Day 4	Carlisle (NY 398 565)	Whitehaven (NX 969 182)	51 miles (82km)	1051m	46

Reivers Route: Three-day itinerary					
	Start	Finish	Distance	Page	
Day 1	Whitehaven (NX 969 182)	Carlisle (NY 398 565)	51 miles (82km)	30	
Day 2	Carlisle (NY 398 565)	Kielder village (NY 626 938)	63 miles (101km)	47	
Day 3	Kielder village (NY 626 938)	Tynemouth (NZ 374 691)	69 miles (111km)	64	

Borderers Ride: Four-day itinerary

	Start	Finish	Distance	Ascent	Page
Day 1	Gretna (NY 316 660)	Bailey Mill (NY 517 785)	35 miles (56km)	640m	92
Day 2	Bailey Mill (NY 517 785)	Bellingham (TQ 374 717)	37 miles (60km)	875m	97
Day 3	Bellingham (TQ 374 717)	Wooler (NT 991 281)	45 miles (72km)	1092m	97
Day 4	Wooler (NT 991 281)	Berwick-upon-Tweed (NU 009 524)	34 miles (55km)	483m	108

Borderers Ride: Three-day itinerary

	Start	Finish	Distance	Page
Day 1	Gretna (NY 316 660)	Kielder village (NY 626 938)	53 miles (85km)	92
Day 2	Kielder village (NY 626 938)	Branton/Ingram area (NU 046 163)	57 miles (92km)	64
Day 3	Branton/Ingram area (NU 046 163)	Berwick-upon-Tweed (NU 009 524)	40 miles (64km)	105

Sunny cycling at Kielder Water (Day 3)

INTRODUCTION

Late afternoon sunlight near Isel in northern Lakeland (Day 1)

The Reivers Route is easily the least ridden of the northern coast-to-coast routes on the National Cycle Network. Yet there is much to be said for the road less travelled. Answering the spirited cry of the adventurer, the Reivers Cycle Route is a wild 170-mile (275km) coast-to-coast ride on cycle paths, little-known minor roads and forest tracks; anyone with a love of cycle touring will delight in this well-kept secret. The ride ventures north from the Cumbrian coast through the dramatic northern fringes of the Lake District National Park and onwards through Carlisle to raid into the wild heart of the thinly populated Border Reivers territory around the England–Scotland border. The route then follows the border through one of Europe's largest forests to reach Kielder Water with its purpose-built cycle path. From there the route continues, incorporating the scenic valleys and airy tops of the Northumberland National Park, often on gated roads that see hardly any motor vehicles. Finally, the ride sweeps south and eastwards to reach Tynemouth for an end sequence of 15 miles on predominantly cinder and tarmac cycle paths.

The Reivers Route was developed by a consortium including Sustrans and opened in 1998, but has seen a series of revisions over the last two decades, with the most recent changes being made in 2020. The original premise was to provide an

Cycling the Reivers Route

extended east-to-west return journey for the ever-popular C2C cycle route and, subsequently, for the increasingly popular Hadrian's Cycleway, both of which end at the mouth of the River Tyne. However, most cyclists who undertake the Reivers Route do so to experience the ride in its own right, usually from west to east. Our primary route description reflects this tendency and describes the route in the Whitehaven to Tynemouth direction, with advice on how to reverse the route at the end of each stage.

WHY CHOOSE THE REIVERS ROUTE?

The Reivers Route is a wilder, hillier and more challenging undertaking than Sustrans' other northern coast-to-coast rides. Its remote sections and superb lengthy off-road passages are part of its appeal. All of this means that the full route is best tackled over four days. The ride is also replete with exceptional cycling, whether it is the meandering line adopted among the watercolour landscapes on the Back o' Skiddaw;

The Reivers Route skirts the England–Scotland border

passing along the England–Scotland border in the enchanting deep forest between Kershope Bridge and Kielder Water on tracks and cinder paths; or rolling along the gated roads that maintain an elevated course over the north-western Pennines between Bellingham and Ponteland. As remote as the Reivers Route at times feels – especially on Days 2 and 3 – amenities have a knack of being at just the right locations.

WHO WERE THE REIVERS?

Picture yourself living near the England–Scotland border 500 years ago. It is the dead of night. A distant sound of pounding hooves chasing over heathery moors is mixing with the howl of wind-driven rain. A raid is imminent. You either flee, lock the door of your bastle house or take to arms in order to defend your land, livestock and family. It is a brutal existence. If raided, you will retaliate with a raid of your own. This is the life of a Border Reiver.

The Border Reivers are most keenly associated with the period between the 13th and 17th centuries – although the borderers were probably a distinct group dating back at least to the Roman partition of Great Britain in the time of Hadrian. As the Borderlands were subjected to the toing and froing of advancing and retreating English and Scottish armies, the Border Reivers emerged as a distinguishable people who carved out an identity distinct from either Scottishness or Englishness. Indeed, in 1525 the Archbishop of Glasgow, Gavin Dunbar, issued a 'Curse of the Reivers and their Descendants', which was to be read from every pulpit and market cross in the Borderlands. The 1000-word curse is terrifying in the vengeance it threatens to wreak on the Reivers: 'All malevolence and curses that ever affected worldly creatures since the beginning of the world to this hour must light upon them.'

The Reivers were hardened by geography and circumstance. As passing armies would exploit and raid, local inhabitants themselves could be paid or inculcated into the warring advances. Likewise the raided were also raiders in their own right, pillaging other Reiver strongholds or foraying farther afield. It was an age of fluid alliances and blood feuds, when kinship meant everything and national affiliation meant very little. Sheep wrangling was often the most prevalent ambition on a raid – 'to reive' is to raid livestock. Wealthier Reivers built bastle houses to defend themselves against other marauding Reivers. Bastles (coming from the familiar French word *bastille*, meaning stronghold) were generally two-storey keeps, although variations of such medieval 'tower houses' can be seen across Europe. The ground floor would house the livestock and the occupants would live upstairs. Over 1000 bastles, often in the form of pele towers, were built in the

Cycling the Reivers Route

Woodhouse Bastle gives a flavour of life in reiving times (Borderers Ride, Day 3)

Borders between 1500 and 1700. Some of these can be seen today on the Reivers Route and the Borderers Ride. But such dwellings could hold out only so long; the razing to the ground of buildings with inhabitants and livestock inside was not uncommon. As you cycle along some of the quietest and wildest minor roads in Britain, often without seeing another soul for hours, it is easy to imagine the spectral figures of long-ago Reivers galloping their way across the moors on one of their raids.

While the union of the crowns of England and Scotland under James I (James VI of Scotland) diminished the contested nature of the border region and the Reivers became less relevant or distinguishable, many would argue that a special Reivers character lives on in the custodians of the region – but if it does, it manifests itself in some of the most warm-hearted and friendly communities in the British Isles. Indeed, Neil Armstrong, who visited Langholm and the pele tower at Gilnockie on an incidental pilgrimage to seek out his roots three years after setting foot on the moon, was reputedly overcome by the good-spirited nature of the border peoples.

The Reivers era left a cultural legacy that extends to a rich vein of poetry and traditional song. Both the valiant and villainous deeds of the period are immortalised in Border ballads. While such ballads give a sense of the troubled times and political realities of the borderlands, they tend to have limited or dubious historical sources and undoubtedly were often written to serve propaganda purposes – whether to invoke anti-English, anti-Scottish or anti-rival clan sentiments. Although the tales were largely invented, these action-packed and often gruesome songs were notably collated by one of Europe's most popular 19th-century authors, Sir Walter Scott, in 1802 (see Appendix C). Many have evolved into folk songs still performed today. A great number of the famous clan families and places on the cycling routes in this book are mentioned in the ballads.

Today, the Reivers Route and the Borderers Ride offer windows into

How tough is the ride?

History is kept alive at the annual Hawick Reivers Festival, usually held in March

the world of the Reivers, which in turn allows an alternative perspective on some of the key contemporary political debates at this fascinating moment in the history of the British Isles, when questions around national identities, Scottish independence and the future of the England–Scotland border abound. To an extent, even the Reiver identity has been swept up into the debate.

HOW TOUGH IS THE RIDE?

The Reivers Route is an attainable goal for most people. If you can comfortably ride 40 miles with 900m of ascent and still clamber back onto your saddle the next day, then you will be more than able to tackle the four-day itinerary. If it were tackled over the same number of days, then the 170-mile Reivers Route would be significantly harder than the 132-mile C2C, the 171-mile Way of the Roses and the 174-mile Hadrian's Cycleway. However, by allowing four days, the Reivers becomes roughly equivalent, if not marginally easier, than those rides tackled over three days. The remote situation of the Kielder Forest traverse is another reason that a four-day itinerary is a sensible choice. The challenge on any cycle tour is naturally increased if planning to carry tents and camping equipment or if prevailing weather conditions work against you.

While the steepest climbs on the Reivers Route are generally found in the northern Lake District, more protracted and equally challenging climbs await in the Borders and Northumbrian segments. These tend to be satisfying affairs that allow height to be savoured once gained. Based on the present OS mapping tool, the overall ascent on the Reivers Route is 3365m. To put this in context, Hadrian's Cycleway has 2378m, the C2C has 3612m and the Way of the Roses has 2829m. The Borderers Ride has 3103m of ascent overall.

A note on the **Kielder Forest traverse:** On our first ride in research for this book we set out from Dalston aiming to make Kielder Water. Late October and carrying full camping kit, our day proved a slow one into north-easterly headwinds. After

Enjoying the purpose-built Lakeside Way around Kielder Water (Day 3)

refuelling in Bailey Mill we began the forest traverse in earnest, confident we would make Kielder Water before nightfall. Optimism about using tyres too narrow for the terrain (see 'What kind of bike?' section) proved misplaced: one of us incurred two punctures, and we only had one suitable spare inner tube. While we were well-equipped and enjoyed the experience of rolling through darkness in heavy driving rain, if your preference is for an easy ride, then entering the forest late in the day is probably not the best plan.

HOW MANY DAYS?

Rather than the three days often afforded for National Cycle Network (NCN) northern England coast-to-coast rides, a four-day itinerary is definitely the best fit for the Reivers Route. Much more so than the other coast-to-coast routes, dividing the Reivers Route into stages is dictated by the availability of accommodation options. A big influencing factor is the scarcity of intermediate stops between Carlisle and Kielder Water, but also to a lesser extent between Bellingham and Maften. Our recommended stop between Carlisle and Kielder Water is at Bailey Mill. This is at the exact halfway point of the overall ride. An important consideration, if aiming to stop overnight in the Kielder Water area, is that Bailey Mill is soon followed by the 12-mile off-road traverse of Kershope and Kielder Forest. This takes you miles from roads and

ALTERNATIVE: THE BORDERERS RIDE

civilisation. The staff at Bailey Mill will happily regale you with tales of tourers who have been benighted in the forest, so careful planning of distances well within your capability is essential. Alternatively, Newcastleton offers a nearby substitute for Bailey Mill. Although 3 miles off route, Newcastleton is visited by the on-road alternative to the forest traverse (see Day 3).

Doing the Reivers Route over the course of three days is a stiff yet feasible challenge for fast cyclists travelling light, but realistically pushes the tricky Kielder Forest traverse to the end of the second day.

While a five-day ride leaves a bit more room to manoeuvre, this itinerary does not fit well with accommodation options to produce sections of similar lengths.

An extensive accommodation list for all itineraries is in Appendix A.

WEST TO EAST OR EAST TO WEST?

Most cyclists undertaking the Reivers Route do so for the route in its own right, rather than as the return leg of the C2C or Hadrian's Cycleway. Respecting this, we describe the Reivers from west to east in order to take advantage of predominant westerlies, although we include a brief description for an east-to-west ride at the end of each stage.

ALTERNATIVE: THE BORDERERS RIDE

The Borderers Ride takes a sensational 150-mile (240km) course which follows the line of the England–Scotland border from coast to coast more closely than that of the Reivers Route. Despite the many merits of the Reivers Route, Sustrans' almost pathological instinct to begin

On the off-road section, following the burn through Kershope Forest (Day 3)

Wordsworth country: Skiddaw, Bassenthwaite and Grisedale Pike (right) (Day 1)

northern coast-to-coast routes on the Cumbrian coast and end them in the Newcastle area means that the opportunity to tailor the Reivers Route more completely towards the border and Reivers' area has been missed. In response to this we have designed the Borderers Ride, which predominantly uses four routes on the National Cycle Network (7, 10, 68 and 1). The Borderers Ride is better suited than the Reivers to a challenging three-day itinerary. It also makes for an easier four-day route than the Reivers. The Borderers Ride incorporates most of Day 2 and all of Day 3 of the Reivers Route, but more logically follows the areas around the England–Scotland border at the beginning and end of the ride in fascinating territory starting in Gretna – nominally at the Lochmaben Stone – and, after incorporating Holy Island, ending in Berwick-upon-Tweed. Although shorter than the Reivers Route, it is similarly challenging and remote. To form logical stages for this guide, the Borderers Ride is divided into four day-sections. That said, the challenging three-day ride is also highly recommended.

GETTING THERE AND BACK

By train

For small groups and solo travellers, the train is a viable and environmentally friendly option that avoids a return to fetch a car. All UK rail operators carry accompanied bikes free of charge, but different operators on your journey may want you to reserve a space for your bike when you book your ticket.

Getting there and back

Whitehaven is connected to the West Coast Main Line at Lancaster and Carlisle by the slow and looping Cumbrian Coast railway line.

It is possible to leave a car in Whitehaven and catch trains back from Newcastle (to get from Tynemouth to Newcastle mainline station, refer to the end of Day 4: Bicycles on the Metro). The Tyne Valley Line connects Newcastle to Carlisle, where a change of trains is necessary to transfer to the Cumbrian Coast railway. The fastest time from Newcastle to Whitehaven is just under three hours. However, be aware – especially if intending to drive home from Whitehaven – that journeys nearer five hours are not uncommon. No reservations are needed to take bikes on these rail routes. While the trains do not have to carry more than two bicycles at a time if they are busy, this seems to be down to the discretion of the staff and no problems have been reported.

The Borderers Ride has straightforward rail access. Gretna is on the West Coast Main Line and Berwick-upon-Tweed is on the East Coast Main Line. To return to Gretna from Berwick, or vice versa, connections that go via Newcastle or Edinburgh take 3–4 hours – the fastest option being dependent on the time and day chosen.

With vehicles and parking

Driving to the start of the route and returning by train at the end is a fairly popular option. Parking at the beginning and end of the route needs a little thought. At Whitehaven, free parking away from the town centre and cycling back in is possible. **Careful consideration of local residents is a priority.** The long-stay car park on Preston Street CA28 9DL (surveilled) is a convenient option; this is on the opposite side of the road from Haven Cycles and the small retail park. It has a daily charge of £6, at the time of going to print. Haven Cycles also offers secure car parking (phone ahead: 01946 63263). The best picking-up point in Tynemouth is the free Priors Haven car park on Pier Road NE30 4DB, but this, like several other free car parks nearby, has a maximum stay of two hours no return. There are paid car parks at the top of the Spanish Battery and on Oxford Street. Residential parking is limited and less than ideal. Secure long-term and overnight parking for £7.50 a day is offered by the multi-storey car park at the Beacon Centre in North Shields (phoning ahead is recommended: 0191 2583909).

For the Borderers Ride, if returning by train it may be possible to leave a vehicle in Gretna station car park. Residential parking should not be overly difficult in Gretna. The motorway services near town have paid long-stay parking and access into town for cyclists. In Berwick, the station has paid parking for up to 72 hours. As of 2020, there are free long-stay car parks at Castlegate, Coxons

CYCLING THE REIVERS ROUTE

Lane and Quayside (see www.visitberwick.com for further details).

Some cycling groups choose to have a support vehicle – a family member or friend who drives to meet them at the end of each day. Support vehicles are strongly discouraged from driving large sections of the actual route as this can be inconsiderate to other cyclists.

With private return transport
This is a good option for larger groups of cyclists. A company takes you and your bikes between Newcastle and Whitehaven either before you start or after you complete the ride. A small number of companies organise a 'package' combining both accommodation and return transport between Whitehaven and Tynemouth. Details of companies currently offering these services are in Appendix B.

By bike
It is worth considering combining the Reivers Route with one of two other classic Sustrans coast-to-coast routes: viable options are Hadrian's Cycleway or the C2C route. Hadrian's Cycleway begins in Ravenglass, but passes through Whitehaven on its route to South Shields or Tynemouth. The C2C, meanwhile, begins in Whitehaven and ends at Tynemouth. For the Borderers Ride, one fantastic option would be a circular week-long tour. From Berwick, you could head south on the NCN 1 Coast and Castles route, then join the Reivers Route by cutting across from Seaton Sluice (avoiding Tyneside). The Reivers could be followed to Bellingham, then the NCN 68 Pennine Cycleway taken south to connect with Hadrian's Cycleway from Gilsland back to Carlisle and Gretna on NCN 7.

WHERE TO STAY
All itineraries for the Reivers Route take account of availability of accommodation. Advanced accommodation booking is recommended, even if camping. There is a limited range of accommodation on certain stretches, in particular the passages between Carlisle and Bailey Mill (or Newcastleton) and also between Bellingham and Maften. On the Reivers Route, a high proportion of cycle tourers choose to camp, embracing the wilder nature of the ride and having the satisfaction of carrying all they need. Campsites on the route are noted in the text and camping is a cheap and viable option for all itineraries in this book.

Bed and breakfast accommodation is also a viable option, although bear in mind that not all serve evening meals. This option saves on weight and the hassle of buying or making breakfast (although the jury is out on whether fry-ups and big hills first thing in the morning are a good mix!). Other budget options such as pubs, hostels, bunkhouses and self-catering are included in the accommodation list where they

The North Tyneside Waggonways are well surfaced and passable on all bikes (Day 4)

are convenient for the route. There has been a proliferation of so-called glamping venues in Northumberland particularly. These have been included where they allow one-night stays. Wild camping is also an option, particularly in Scottish territory where it is legal in many places, and there is even a bothy deep in the dark secluded Kielder Forest – if you dare! (See Day 3.) A detailed list of accommodation along the ride is given in Appendix A. It is worth noting that Bailey Mill is given as an overnight stop for a four-day Reivers or Borderers ride. There is only one choice here, but the accommodation on site includes B&B, self-catering and camping. It also serves evening meals and sells packed lunches.

With the exception of the first 11 miles, Day 1 of the Borderers Ride follows the same route as Day 2 of the Reivers Route, and Day 2 corresponds with Day 3 of the Reivers. Therefore, much of the accommodation is the same for both rides. Campsites and YHAs at Wooler and Berwick are also useful for this route.

WHAT KIND OF BIKE?

The Reivers is a route on mixed terrain and some thought should be given to your bike. **Rugged touring bikes**, sturdy **hybrid bikes** and **gravel bikes** with more than 42mm tyres are ideal for tackling both the off- and on-road sections of the Reivers and Borderers, especially if carrying luggage.

Mountain bikes are not suitable for the Reivers and Borderers cycle tours as the majority of the miles are done on tarmac.

The off-road sections of the Reivers are sometimes rocky, muddy

BEFORE SETTING OFF ON YOUR BIKE

If, like us, there are limits to your mechanical expertise, then it is well worth taking your bike to the local shop for a pre-Reivers service. For the cost – which might only be £20 if everything is in order – weigh up the inconvenience of having to do any major running repairs en route or having to quit the ride. Make sure that your bike is set up correctly – you will be on it for long consecutive stretches.

and loose. They are definitely not suitable for **road bikes**. That said, road cyclists should not be put off – although the off-road forest and lakeshore sections are highlights of the Reivers, great on-road alternatives to all the tricky sections are described in the text and mean the Reivers is still a worthwhile tour on a road bike.

Experienced **tandemists** should be able to stay in the saddle with a few exceptions – the Kielder Forest and Lakeside Way passages of the ride would be most challenging. The willingness of rail operators to accept tandems on trains and the space and provision for them varies. As well as checking with rail operators when planning your journey, the Tandem Club's website (www.tandem-club.org.uk) gives a good breakdown of what the existing rules are. National Express coaches may accept tandems and can prove an alternative to rail.

Electric bikes: Familiarity with the specific capability of your eBike and planning ahead on how its battery might be recharged is crucial. The logistical challenge of the sparsely populated Reivers Route makes it a less eBike-friendly outing than other routes, such as Hadrian's Cycleway.

EQUIPMENT

Ensure you do not forget the following:
- bike lights
- bell
- spare inner tube or tubes
- tyre levers
- pump
- Allen keys
- puncture repair kit
- small first aid kit
- a lightweight bike lock may be useful

Hydration and emergency energy food are crucial on this ride as opportunities to fill up and stock up are limited. Carry two-litre bottles in frame cages and plenty of calories. This is particularly important on Day 2 and Day 3 of the Reivers (Day 1 and 2 of the Borderers), where amenities are sparse. Plan ahead carefully, particularly on the section from Carlisle (or Longtown) to Bailey Mill. On this 35-mile section there are remarkably no shops or cafés and only one pub, which may be closed during the day.

CARRYING YOUR GEAR

In cycle touring, travelling light is a top priority.

Panniers are a long-standing good choice for cycle tourers. A rack frame is needed in order to use them. Some form of frame can be fitted to most types of bike. Cyclists carrying lots of camping equipment might add front panniers. If you have never ridden with panniers before, it is advisable to do a few practice rides fully loaded before you set out on a multi-day tour.

Saddle packs with capacities up to 17 litres can reduce wind resistance and are amazingly simple storage for those able to travel light. Other saddle bags, seat packs, triangular frame bags and handlebar bags can also be good options to provide extra accessible storage.

Heavy rucksacks should be **avoided** but a small daysack could be a viable option for those travelling light.

WHAT TO WEAR

Helmets

We recommend them – they are obviously beneficial in the event of an accident or collision, but it comes down to personal preference. There is no current UK law forcing cyclists to wear helmets. In their favour, helmets are now lightweight, allow airflow to the head and can hide bald patches!

Clothing

Most people will find that cycling-specific clothing is useful. Cycling shorts or tights are padded in the right areas and improve comfort

Well equipped for a cycle tour in the wild Borderlands

Tynemouth Priory and Castle above King Edward's Bay (Day 4)

during long days in the saddle. Cycling jerseys usually have several useful features: high-visibility colours, reflective strips, dropped backs to avoid a draughty gap and easily accessible back pockets – it's amazing how much gear and food you can cram into these. Waterproof, windproof and thermal layers are also especially important due to the remote nature of this ride. Many feel cycling gloves give better grip and reduce handlebar vibration. They are a very good idea outside of summer, as is an earband. Cycling glasses are especially useful if prone to runny eyes or wearing contact lenses.

Footwear

Footwear is a matter of personal choice: most types of trainer will suffice for the Reivers Route, although specific cycling shoes are an option. Many seasoned cycle tourers swear by the carrying of Crocs or flip-flops to change into for evening relaxation.

MAPS AND APPS

The maps in this book, along with the detailed route descriptions, should provide everything you need to do the Reivers Route and Borderers Ride. In line with the National Cycle Network, these maps indicate which sections are traffic-free.

For those who prefer electronic maps, due to the remote nature of the ride and lack of consistent mobile signal, we advise downloading mapping in advance and taking this book or a paper map as a backup. A Footprint map of the route is available at the same scale as the maps in this book (1:100,000). The official route has been changed only slightly since the most recent 2013 edition.

For those who wish to have more detailed mapping, the Reivers is covered at 1:50,000 scale by the following OS Landranger sheets: 89, 85, 90, 86, 79, 80, 87 and 88. The Borderers is covered on 74, 75 and 85. The Ordnance Survey now offers access to all its British maps on computers and mobile devices for a small fee. Other apps such as ViewRanger allow users to access parts of OS mapping for a small fee and use OpenCycleMap to provide larger-scale free maps.

Note that a 2019 map of the 'Reivers Cycle Routes', is not suitable for use with this book. The map does not show the official Sustrans route with blue National Cycle Network signage which we describe. As explained further in 'Signage', it is best to ignore signs for these routes while using this guidebook.

SIGNAGE

The Reivers Route is signed with the small blue pointer signs of the National Cycle Network, mainly showing the route number '10'

An official Reivers Route '10' sign heading into Kershope Forest (Day 3)

(although some short sections are on routes 71, 7, 68 and 72). As of 2020, there were signs at most significant junctions going west to east. However, the Reivers Route has not seen as much investment and promotion as some of the other popular NCN routes and the clarity of the signage has suffered in parts, particularly as the route has been altered on a number of occasions. **On Day 4, the route through the Backworth area near Newcastle has seen several adjustments** – close reading of the guidebook is useful. Signs take the form of blue stickers bearing '10' on lampposts and road sign posts. We have highlighted areas where close attention must be paid to navigation.

While using this guidebook, ignore any unofficial badges with crossed swords. Confusingly labelled 'Reivers Routes', these belong to two independent and alternative on and off-road versions of a cycle route between Maryport and Tynemouth. They are not overseen by Sustrans nor are they part of the National Cycle Network. When the authors last contacted Sustrans about this, negotiations were underway in order to allay this confusion.

USING THIS GUIDE

The Reivers Route is described in detail in four stages. Each has a summary of what to expect on the day ahead, along with a comprehensive route description and detailed maps, at a smaller scale where the route goes through populated areas. Points at which it is important to pay attention to the navigation are highlighted, as well as potential hazards. Details of worthwhile variations are given at the appropriate points within the text, and descriptions of any road-bike-friendly alternatives to off-road sections are provided. Also included in each day section is a route profile, showing where the main climbs and descents of the day take place.

Route information boxes for each stage provide everything you need to know before going on the ride, such as mileage, ascent and refreshment stops. Total ascents are approximate and the gradients refer to the steepest parts of the climbs. Although details of distances, ascents, stops and refreshments are given, cyclists should refer to the main text for detailed description of the route.

GPX tracks

GPX tracks for the routes in this guidebook are available to download free at www.cicerone.co.uk/910/GPX. GPX files are provided in good faith, but neither the authors nor the publisher accept responsibility for their accuracy.

THE REIVERS ROUTE: THE FOUR-DAY RIDE

Climbing the challenging Fairspring Banks to Ryal (Day 4)

Binsey looms over the road near Bewaldeth (Day 1)

THE REIVERS ROUTE: THE FOUR-DAY RIDE

The beauty of the Reivers Route is its contrasting days. The first is a collage of short sharp hill climbs interspersed with glorious downhills and steadier flatter sections. From Whitehaven the route shares its course briefly with Hadrian's Cycleway before heading inland to Cockermouth to discover the secret treasures of the northern Lake District. On this day, good lunch and tearoom stops can be found in Great Broughton, Cockermouth and the splendid village of Hesket Newmarket – an especially popular stop with cyclists. The most logical overnight stop is in historic Carlisle, with its close Reiver associations.

The second day's climbs are far more gradual and the roads soon become quiet to the point of feeling remote. After crossing the M6, the wild beauty of the Reivers territory becomes apparent. From Carlisle until the end of the day when the oasis of the Bailey Mill B&B pub complex near the Scottish border is reached, not a single shop or café is passed and the sole pub en route at Hethersgill tends not to open during the day. This lack of amenities should not be disconcerting; tearooms must wait another day, for there is something special hereabouts. Good indoor breaks can nevertheless be had at the free museum and church at Bewcastle and the church at Kirklinton (toilet). As long as provisions are bought in Carlisle, then the remoteness of this day will just make

THE REIVERS ROUTE: THE FOUR-DAY RIDE

the pint and meal awaiting in Bailey Mill all the more satisfying. Bailey Mill has the motto 'always open and willing to help'; it sells onward food and packed lunches for the beginning of Day 3. Along with B&Bs near Kershope Bridge, Newcastleton is another viable overnight stop which has the distinction of being in Scotland.

The Reivers third day is an adventurous affair that is predominantly off-road (an on-road alternative via Newcastleton is also described). On meeting the Scottish border at Kershope Bridge, tarmac is exchanged for rough forest tracks which at Kielder Water give way to a well-surfaced pleasant lakeside cycle track. Quiet minor roads dominate the final stretch from Falstone to Bellingham. Good lunchbreaks on the third day can be found beside Kielder Water at Leaplish Waterside Park and Tower Knowe, and also in Falstone. Bellingham is a great large village with plentiful accommodation.

The fourth day involves a long climb to a lofty situation on the Pennine tops and some of the best cycling roads in the country – albeit with lots of gates! These lead eventually to Maften – an ideal lunch stop. From Maften the route descends through Ponteland, then bypasses the majority of Newcastle proper, largely on surfaced cycle paths and former mining railway lines to the city's north. The last stretch deploys mainly secluded cycle paths to ingeniously negotiate the urban sprawl that leads enjoyably to a finish on the clifftops overlooking the North Sea at Tynemouth.

The wonderful path round Kielder Water is well surfaced (Day 3)

CYCLING THE REIVERS ROUTE

DAY 1
Whitehaven to Carlisle

Start	Whitehaven (NX 969 182)
Finish	Carlisle (NY 398 565)
Distance	51 miles (82km)
Total ascent	1076m
Steepest climb	'Back o' Skiddaw' area has some gems: the short sharp shock up to Fell End on the slopes of Binsey comes out of nowhere and touches 1 in 5 on its hairpin; the climb through Lowthwaite Farm is also fairly stiff; while the two steep sections of the protracted ascent from Longlands Beck will probably challenge most.
Terrain	There are good surfaces on the traffic-free paths on the coast. The day's ride is all possible on a road bike. The section from Cockermouth onwards is all on quiet minor roads.
OS maps	Landranger 89, 90 and 85
Refreshments	Workington, Great Broughton, Cockermouth, Hesket Newmarket, Dalston
Intermediate distances	Workington 8 miles (13km), Great Broughton 12 miles (19km), Cockermouth 15 miles (24km), Longlands 26 miles (42km), Caldbeck 32 miles (51km), Hesket Newmarket 34 miles (55km)

The day starts with a superb stretch of sea-view riding along traffic-free paths on the Cumbrian coast. A well-maintained network of disused rail lines takes you through Workington and then inland towards the Lakeland fells, which form the skyline for a large section of the ride. The route then heads through the attractive market town of Cockermouth – birthplace of William and Dorothy Wordsworth – and skirts the tranquil north-western fringes of the Lake District National Park, threading a course round the Back o' Skiddaw – with views of the eponymous mountain providing some of the day's scenic highlights. Hilly terrain dominates this section until the route approaches the tamer Caldew valley and eventually reaches the large,

Day 1 – Whitehaven to Carlisle

unassuming village of Dalston. For campers, there is a good site between here and Carlisle, but for other cycle tourers we would recommend carrying on for a further five flat and mainly traffic-free miles to stay in the historic cathedral city and Cumbrian county town of Carlisle.

Although some cyclists start the Reivers Route at the C2C harbour sculpture, the official beginning is intended to be at the nearby Beacon area. The Beacon, which now houses a local history museum, is the cone-topped white cylindrical building at the south side of the main harbour. The most dramatic and fitting start point is at the lookout, by the Candlestick chimney on the bluffs above this. The harbour is easily reached from Whitehaven rail station: cycle out of the car park past a superstore and turn right on the main road into town. Take the first left (10 signage), then cut left almost immediately onto the seafront path.

The distinctive **Candlestick chimney** vented a mineshaft of the former Wellington Pit, the scene of Cumbria's worst mining disaster, in which 134 miners lost their lives in 1910. There are two monuments to the tragedy here, along with a recently commissioned mosaic. It is a contemplative and scenic spot to start the ride.

Whitehaven's Candlestick chimney and the Beacon from one of the town's two lighthouses

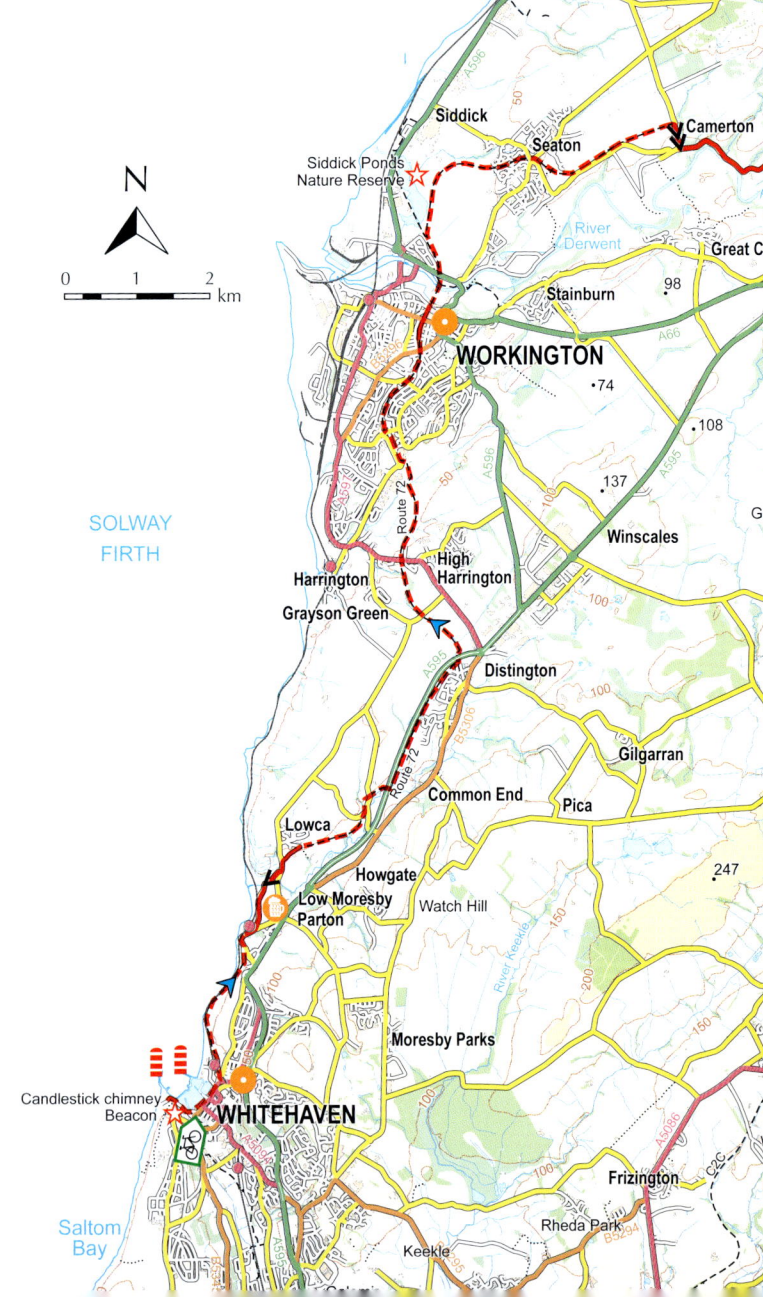

Day 1 – Whitehaven to Carlisle

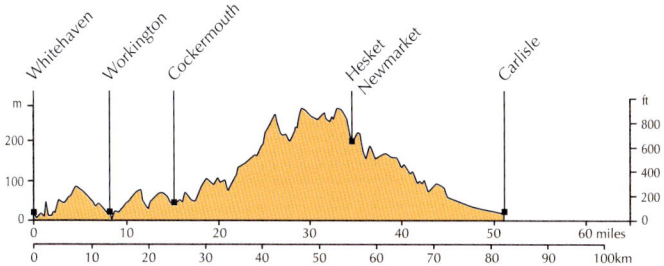

The **Candlestick** is reached easily by cycling alongside the harbour and zigzagging a cyclable path up from the car park by the Beacon. There is a large 'C2C' sculpture by the water's edge on the first slipway at NX 971 182 that marks the start of that route; it is a suitable place to dip a wheel in the Irish Sea. ▶

From Whitehaven to just outside of Workington, the Reivers Route shares its course with another excellent Sustrans ride, Hadrian's Cycleway.

Whitehaven has a rich **sea-faring history**, recognised by its maritime museum and an annual festival. In 1778 the town was attacked by the proto US Navy commanded by John Paul Jones during the American War of Independence. The historical importance of **mining** in the region explains why many of the cycle paths occupy former mining railways.

From the Beacon area, cycle around the harbourside path past docks until the path finishes at a seaweed sculpture. Here turn right and then left briefly onto a busy town road. Turn off this, taking a left uphill after the petrol station, signed as the 10, but immediately fork left onto a dead-end road. This soon becomes a paved cycle path beside the rail line and affords great sea views. The Dumfries and Galloway hills can be seen across the Solway Firth on most days.

The excellent coastal path continues for over a mile around Tanyard Bay, then briefly dips down through the village of **Parton**. Turn left at the T-junction and follow the road through the village, which eventually climbs fairly

Map continues on page 36

Poised above the railway and below the sandstone cliffs of Tanyard Bay

A German U-boat fired on Parton, Harrington and Whitehaven in August 1915.

steeply to another T-junction. Turn left, but take a right turn in 100 metres. ◄

The route cuts immediately left through awkward barriers onto a cycle path over a small recreation area, but continuing straight ahead onto the gravelly road is far simpler. At the top of this, turn right, being careful to soon take a left fork onto a cycle path which takes a disused rail line for 4 miles via **Distington**, before the edge of **Workington** is reached, with little complication. Take a signed left at a T-junction of paths towards Workington.

WORKINGTON

The proud town of Workington is the home of 'Uppies and Downies': an idiosyncratic sport played only in Workington. The 'Uppies' are participants traditionally resident in the slightly more affluent upper area of the town while the 'Downies' are those whom – historically at least – would have been resident in the reclaimed marshes, dockland and coastal dwellings. Matches have been recorded as far back as the 16th century and are still played annually. They involve upwards of 1000 players trying to move a ball – usually by means of a scrum – to the opposition's 'goal' across town; this often takes hours.

Day 1 – Whitehaven to Carlisle

The route now skirts around Workington Fire Station, where it briefly adopts a shared-use pavement before trending right onto more secluded disused rail line to the town centre. The path emerges at a car park. Head straight on (passing town centre shops and cafés to your right) and go downhill through a short tunnel, after which a plethora of cycling signage appears. The Reivers Route meets the alternative eastbound start of the C2C route here.

Head straight on, rejoining the rail path, crossing the **River Derwent**. Continue for a further 700 metres, to a junction of paths. Here, Hadrian's Cycleway forks off left, but our route goes straight on (as does the alternative C2C), following yet more pleasant rail line through **Siddick Ponds Nature Reserve** and **Seaton** to emerge at a minor road above Camerton, where the Lakeland fells (most noticeably the Skiddaw massif) become more prominent in the distance. ▶

Turn right steeply downhill through the village of **Camerton**, being careful not to miss a sharp left turn midway down the hill. Take this undulating minor road, initially following the course of the **River Derwent**, to **Great Broughton** (pubs, café, shop). Bear right onto the main street towards Cockermouth and continue straight through the village, in 200 metres taking a left – effectively straight on – towards Papcastle. ▶

Continue on the winding narrow road through **Papcastle** to the **A5086**. Look for a path opposite (just to the right of the factory gates). Cross the A5086 with care and take the path, bearing right when it ends then almost immediately taking a similar path down the side of a car park and over a footbridge to enter **Cockermouth** and reach Main Street, with its independent shops and places to eat.

Turn left up Main Street to cross an easily missed bridge over the River Cocker, which gives the town its name. Ignore signage pointing off right for the C2C or 71 and instead go straight ahead uphill on Castlegate (signed as the 10). The privately owned Cockermouth Castle can be glimpsed through gates to the left.

The Siddick Ponds reserve is one of the best places in Cumbria to spot otters.

Remains of a substantial Roman fort were discovered at Papcastle near the sharp bend in the River Derwent.

COCKERMOUTH

Cockermouth, home of Jennings Brewery, lies just outside the Lake District National Park boundary. Poets William and Dorothy Wordsworth spent their early years here. While Cockermouth does not become overwhelmed by summer tourist hoards, the National Trust-owned Georgian Wordsworth House on Main Street attracts plenty of visitors. Cockermouth was badly hit by floods in 2009; an interesting consequence of the devastation was the discovery of the remains of a large Roman civilian settlement in the vicinity, associated with the nearby Roman fort of Derventio. Fletcher Christian, the most famous mutineer on the *Bounty*, called Cockermouth home, as did cricketer Ben Stokes, who learnt his trade at the local club.

Take a left at the end of the castle boundary wall onto Isel Road. This soon leaves town to provide another undulating and scenic passage. After 3 miles, turn left downhill to cross **Isel Bridge** over the River Derwent.

After crossing, immediately go right signed to Sunderland and Bewaldeth. Continue for a further mile, with views of the Skiddaw and Uldale fells beginning to dominate the horizon. In a mile, take the next right fork towards Bewaldeth. This is a superb stretch of single-track road with Bassenthwaite Lake creeping into view to the south. Continue for 2 miles to cross – with care – the **A591** and head into **Bewaldeth**, bearing left to go through the small village.

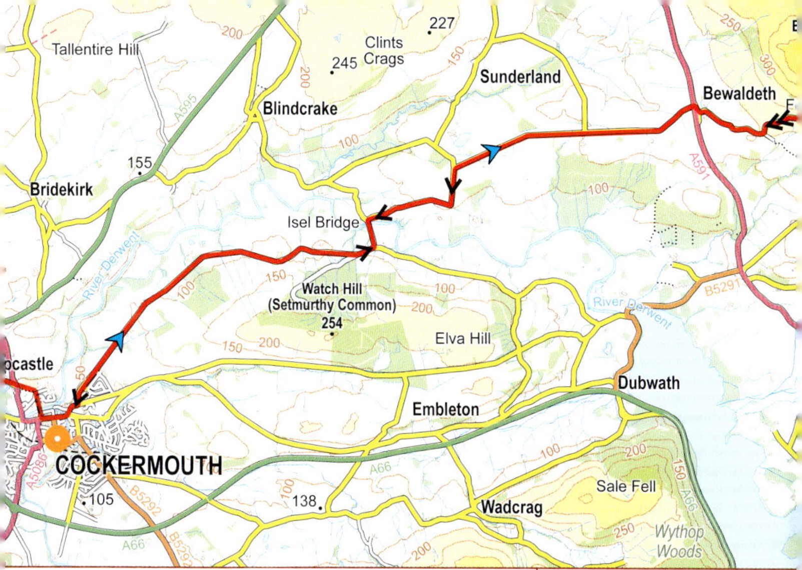

Continue, with some surprisingly fierce climbing across the southern fellside of Binsey (447m), to pass

Map continues on page 38

Skiddaw from the road to Over Water

through the hamlet of **Fell End**. Tough though this climb is, the added height gained provides classic views of the higher Lakeland fells.

Go right at a T-junction and immediately merge right again, then 150 metres later look out for a left turn to Over Water at the bottom of the steep hill. This is a quiet corner of the Lake District known as Back o' Skiddaw and the mountain looms large to the right as you pass the shapely little lake of **Over Water**. ◄

> Over Water is the third largest Lake District tarn and is used to supply drinking water to Wigton.

The road swings right after the tarn and 300 metres later turn left towards Caldbeck, passing **Chapelhouse Reservoir** and climbing to the hamlet of **Lowthwaite**. Two options are now possible.

For the primary route, dip over a bridge only to ascend to the hamlet of **Longlands** – another tough climb which peaks at 282m just after a cattle grid on a shallow saddle between Longlands and Aughtertree fells. A further kilometre on exposed moorland brings

Map continues on page 40

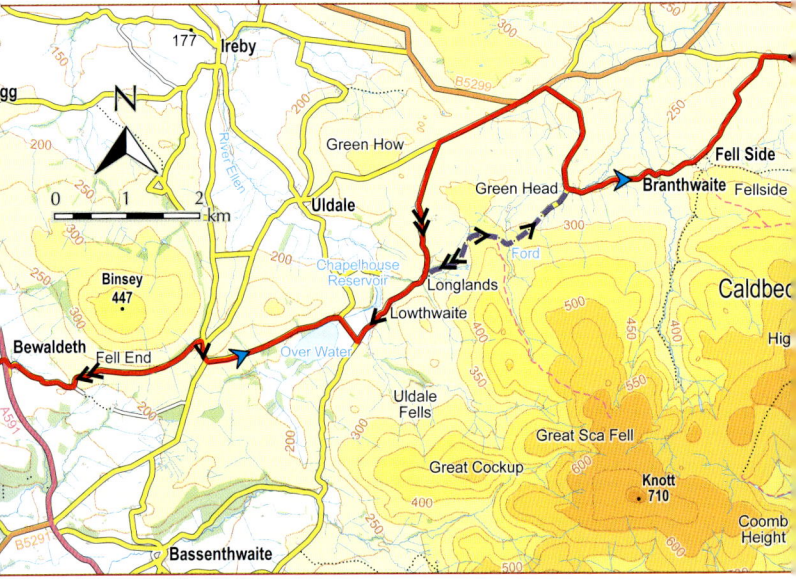

The bridge at Green Head on the Back o' Skiddaw

you to a T-junction; here turn right towards Caldbeck and descend gradually on a briefly busier stretch of road. Look out for a right turn to Green Head and Fell Side and take this onto another stunning stretch through the hamlets of **Green Head**, **Branthwaite** and, after a further climb, **Fell Side**.

Off-road alternative to Green Head

For a tough off-road alternative, dip over the bridge just before Longlands and take the bridleway track immediately on the right to climb, gaining 100m of height, over a shoulder of Longlands Fell. After crossing Charleton Wath **ford** in descent, the primary route is rejoined at a T-junction beside **Green Head**, where a right turn is followed by a bridge in 100 metres. Continue through **Branthwaite** and on up to **Fell Side**.

After a further mile on high ground, turn left at the next T-junction and descend steeply, passing a turning for Caldbeck (the pretty village is 1km off route but has cafés and a pub). Just over an undulating mile later comes

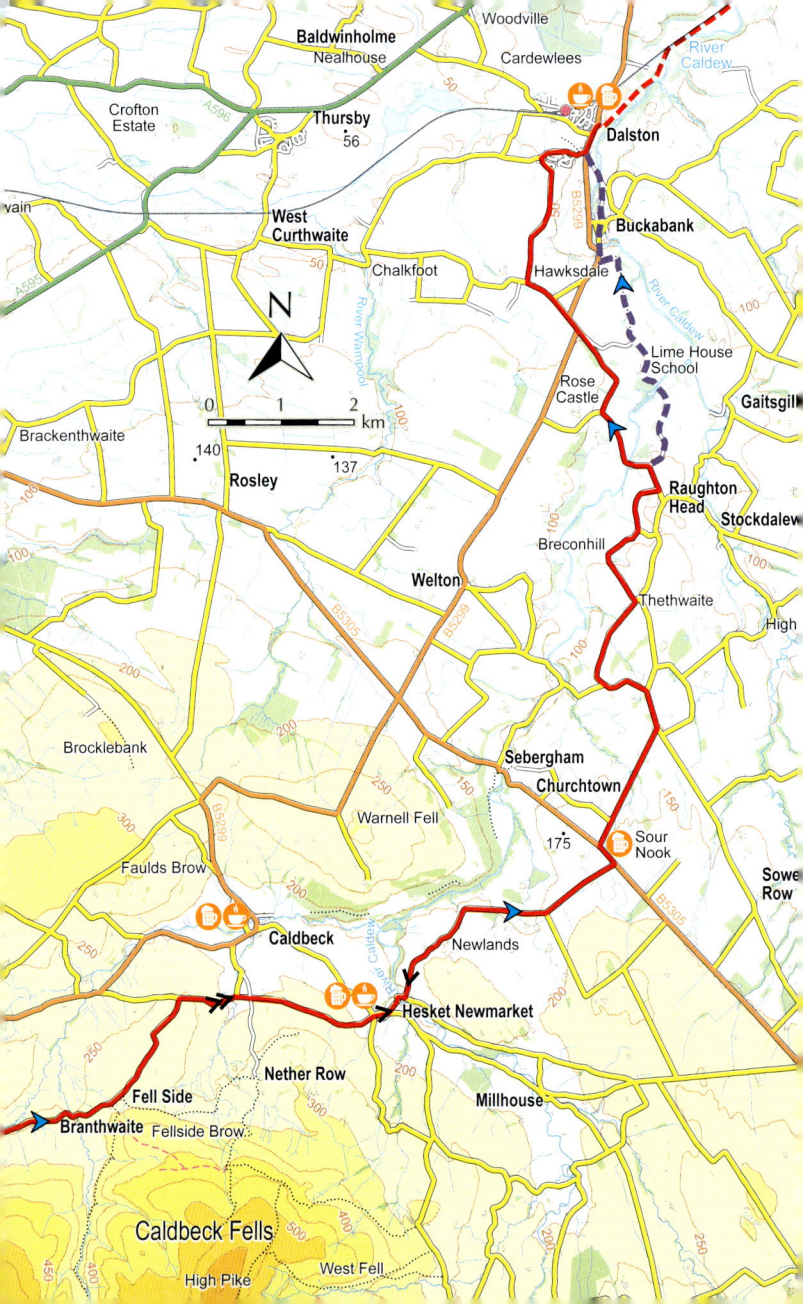

Day 1 – Whitehaven to Carlisle

another rest option in the shape of **Hesket Newmarket** (pub, and café in the village shop).

Fork left out of the village centre opposite the Old Crown pub onto a steep and winding descent to cross the **River Caldew**. Climb back up again to **Newlands** hamlet and then the road flattens out to meet the **B5305** in 2 miles. Here take care turning left and then, after 200 metres, right by the **Sour Nook** pub, signed to Raughton Head. There is now a sense of having left the Lake District proper behind.

Map continues on page 42

> **Note:** Over the years, Sustrans have added and then removed untidy off-road alternatives in the area between Sour Nook and Dalston, including one route via the hamlet of Churchtown. Old signs can cause confusion.

In a further mile, the Reivers Route is joined by NCN Route 7 (which can be followed all the way up the western coast of Scotland and onwards to Inverness). Half a mile later, turn left towards Welton and Bellbridge on a narrower road. Continue straight on through farming country, ignoring the first left at a triangular junction to reach the hamlet of **Thethwaite** in 1km. Here, turn left, soon reaching **Breconhill**.

Follow the road rightwards through the hamlet then keep straight on until a left turn at the church in **Raughton Head** can be taken. Shortly after this, an off-road alternative leaves to go up Raughtonhead Hill to the right.

At the time of writing, both NCN routes 7 and 10 shared this off-road route and the main on-road route into Dalston. The road route is easy and allows a glimpse of Rose Castle, whereas the off-road option (details to follow) has trickier route-finding and can often be muddy.

For the road option continue straight ahead and descend to cross the **River Caldew** on Rose Bridge. Fork right 500 metres later at **Rose Castle**.

The fortifications at **Rose Castle** were home to the bishops of Carlisle for nearly 800 years. The oldest part of the building is the pele tower known as Strickland's Tower. Despite being the scene of repeated burnings by Scots and being attacked during the English Civil War, Rose Castle now functions as a peace study centre. It is not open to visitors but can be seen from the road or public footpath through its grounds.

Continue a further mile to turn (carefully) right onto the **B5299** at a T-junction. After 200 metres turn off left towards Curthwaite and Wigton. Pass through a hamlet and take the second signed right turn to Dalston and Carlisle (if in doubt, there was NCN 7 Reivers signage here in 2020 and a 7.5t traffic weight limit). This road leads easily to a T-junction on the outskirts of **Dalston**. Turn right through housing to reach Dalston's main street at shops, and turn left here.

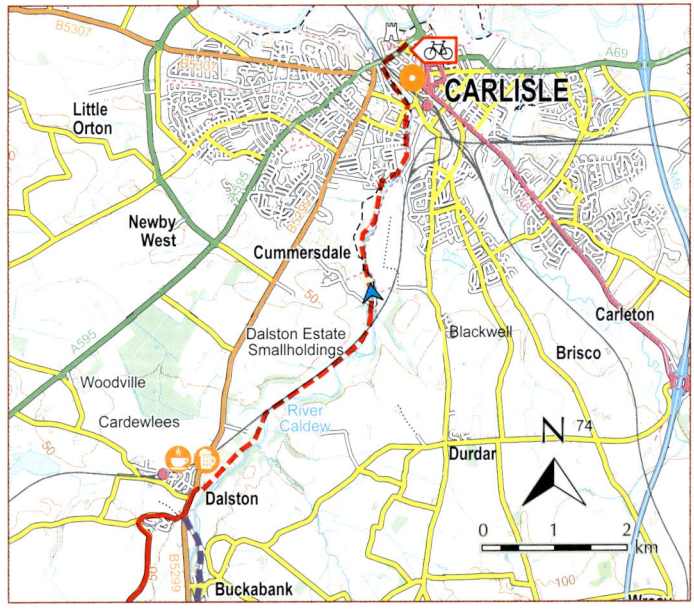

For the off-road route into Dalston

Turn right to Raughtonhead Hill Farm then continue onto a rough and muddy track. Turn left after 400 metres on a track over the **River Caldew**, then through woods to emerge at the well-hidden **Lime House Public School**, where the route joins the Cumbria Way. The track crosses the school's drive and continues to meet a small road. Take this right for a short distance to **Hawksdale Hall**, where there is a gate and the road becomes a track. This crosses fields for just over a mile before emerging onto the **B5299**. Turn right on this for 50 metres then fork right on a busy minor road signed to the M6. After only 100 metres fork left off this on a road called Riverside in the small village of **Buckabank**. Turn right in another 100 metres at the next junction, then 50 metres later take the second left just after a small bridge on a road with a bridleway sign. Follow this well-surfaced path for 500 metres beside a stream to cross the **River Caldew** finally into **Dalston**. Turn right onto Dalston's main street to join the road route.

After turning onto Dalston's main street, continue for 200 metres. (Or, if you're camping, continue for 150 metres, take the left turn out of Dalston and go up Barras

Mural at Cummersdale Holmes

Lane for just under a mile to reach Cardewlees campsite.) Look for a signed but easily missed path on the right down the side of a primary school, beside a recreation ground. This leads first by the **River Caldew** and then beside the rail line.

After 2 miles the path crosses under the railway and follows the river and Cumbria Way into the centre of Carlisle, through the riverside meadows of **Cummersdale Holmes** past a weir on the outskirts of town at Denton Holme. The path crosses onto the eastern side of the river, then emerges at a roadside shared-use path beside the busy **A595**. Go briefly left on this to reach the crossing point and then double back right on the opposite roadside to reach **Carlisle Castle**. ◄

The Tullie House Museum opposite Carlisle Castle has a permanent gallery dedicated to the Border Reivers.

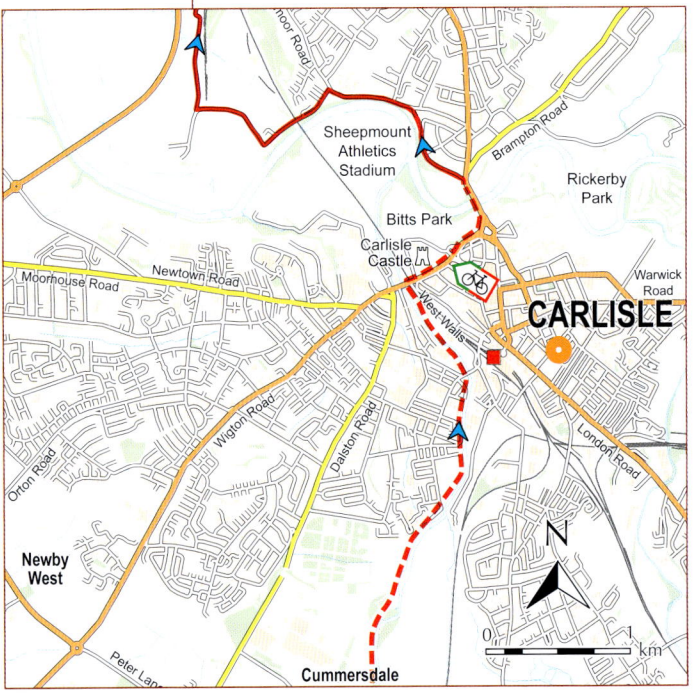

DAY 1 – WHITEHAVEN TO CARLISLE

CARLISLE

Carlisle Castle

Carlisle is the only city in Cumbria and is sometimes referred to as the Great Border City. It has a long and varied Reiver association. In 1525, a Scottish archbishop put a curse on all the Border Reivers. For Carlisle's Millennium celebrations in 2000, the city council thought it a good idea to have the 1000-word curse carved as an artwork onto a granite boulder. Some blamed the carving for the city's post-millennial flooding – more likely to do with climate change or poor river management. The stone can still be seen in an underpass by the castle.

Carlisle Castle is a key site in Border history, being of strategic importance in an area disputed by the English and Scots. The castle was first built on the former Roman site of Luguvalium by William Rufus (son of William the Conqueror) in 1092 in order to secure Cumberland's incorporation into England. There were numerous raids and Scottish attempts to regain the land, giving it the title of most frequently besieged place in Britain.

Carlisle became the seat of the Western March – it later housed March Warden Richard Duke of Gloucester, who went on to become the much-maligned Richard III. The castle was famously a site of Mary Queen of Scots' imprisonment at the hands of her cousin Elizabeth I in 1567 – from which the castle's Queen Mary's Tower gains its name. Mary was allowed to stretch her legs under supervision in the grounds at the front of the castle, now called Lady's Walk. The Reivers still exerted powerful influence in the late Elizabethan period and the notorious Scottish Reiver Kinmont Willie Armstrong was captured in 1596 (somewhat illegally) and imprisoned at Carlisle. Armstrong was broken out of confinement with the help of the bold Buccleuch (the Keeper of Liddesdale) along with the help of reiving families from south of the border such as the Grahams and Carletons. This episode is colourfully recounted in 'The Ballad of Kinmont Willie'. The affair prompted a dispute between James VI of Scotland and Queen Elizabeth. When James ascended to the English throne as James I, and united the crowns in 1603, the castle became a staging point for James' relentless pursuit of Reiver families.

The castle again saw conflict during the Civil War, when Charles I's soldiers were starved out by Scots and Parliamentarian forces. In 1745 during the Second Jacobite Rising, Charles Edward Stuart's forces seized the castle for the Scots, before the English bloodily took it back under William Augustus, the Duke of Cumberland (son of George II). The castle housed Border Regiments until 1959. Today the castle is run by English Heritage (£12.60, free to members) and is home to exhibitions and a Museum of Military Life, as well as being used by the Territorial Army.

EAST TO WEST

This day is equally satisfying, if not equally testing, going from the east. The route out of Dalston needs careful navigation if the off-road option is taken. Height is gained steadily from Dalston up to the loftier terrain around Hesket Newmarket. Thereafter the climb between Hesket Newmarket and Fell Side is nothing short of brutal – a gruelling 1 in 5 at some points. Be thankful though that the more troublesome west-to-east climbs are missed out in this direction. There is a steep pull up from Over Water to the slopes of Binsey. In compensation, the views of the Skiddaw massif are equally good, if not better than in the opposite direction. Later in the day, the climb up from Camerton is testing to the point of being fierce, especially four days into a tour. The last 10 miles are steady, with just a few minor inclines to negotiate. Leaving the central shopping area of Workington, dip under the railway bridge and continue on Central Way to a dead end where a shared-use cycle path continues the route straight on to Whitehaven.

DAY 2
Carlisle to Bailey Mill

Start	Carlisle (NY 398 565)
Finish	Bailey Mill (NY 517 785) or Newcastleton (NY 484 877)
Distance	34 miles (55km); or 41 miles (66km) to Newcastleton
Total ascent	683m; or 857m to Newcastleton
Steepest climb	Through Bewcastle to Park Head farm there is just over a mile of climbing. The pull up from Bewcastle peaks at a tough but rewarding 1 in 6 gradient.
Terrain	Minor roads, sometimes with patchy surfaces, particularly after Bewcastle. All passable on road bikes.
OS maps	Landranger 85, 86 and 79
Refreshments	The Crown and Thistle near Rockcliffe, and the Black Lion at Hethersgill (tel 01228 675318) which is open all day on weekends but not until 3.30pm on weekdays. (Note: as of 2020, the most widely available printed Reivers Route map showed some refreshment options in this section or just off route, which no longer exist.) A seasonal café in Kirklinton Hall just off route may also open. **Be sure to stock up on provisions for the day.**
Intermediate distances	Westlinton 10 miles (16km), Kirklinton 15 miles (24km), Hethersgill 19 miles (31km), Kirkcambeck 23 miles (37km), Bewcastle 29 miles (47km)

The highlight of Day 2's riding is undoubtedly the superb passage onwards from Kirkcambeck, where the wild Northumberland moors and undulating roads seemingly lead into the middle of nowhere to reach the lonely and romantically situated hamlet of historic Bewcastle, with its Roman and Reivers associations, mini-museum, ruins and ornate Anglo-Saxon cross. It is crucial to plan ahead carefully for the day: from the Carlisle vicinity to Bailey Mill there are remarkably no shops or cafés, while the pub at Hethersgill cannot be relied upon on weekdays. Although the distance involved in this stage seems modest, rest assured that there is significant height gain in the second half of the day that can sometimes be exposed and windy. Bailey Mill or Newcastleton (for those taking the on-road option on Day 3 or a spur off the main route) provide the logical places to stop in this increasingly remote section of the ride. Pushing on to Kielder Water is of course an option, but it makes a lot of sense to tackle the challenging section through Kielder Forest with fresh legs and time on your side on Day 3.

Map continues on page 51

From the front of **Carlisle Castle** continue on the shared-use pavement (a road sign marks the North and A7). This pavement leads leftwards across a large roundabout then beside the A7. Cross the **River Eden**. After 150 metres, take the first left onto the quiet Cavendish Terrace. This culminates in a dead end at a short snicket (dismount). Emerging from the snicket, go left along Etterby Street, taking another left after 400 metres onto Etterby Road to cross the rail line and leave the city behind.

After 500 metres, bear right at a triangular T-junction. Less than a mile ahead, carefully use cycle paths and crossings to negotiate a roundabout on the A689 heading straight on to **Rockcliffe**, which is reached quickly after 2½ miles and just one filtered left turn. In the attractive village, dip down a dead-end road at the left of St Mary's Church to cross a beck. This area, alongside the mouth of the River Eden where it empties into the tidal Solway Firth, is known as the Rockcliffe Coast, only 3 miles from the border with Scotland.

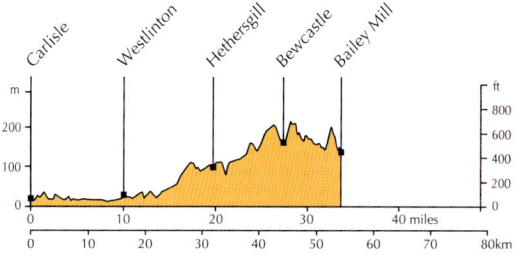

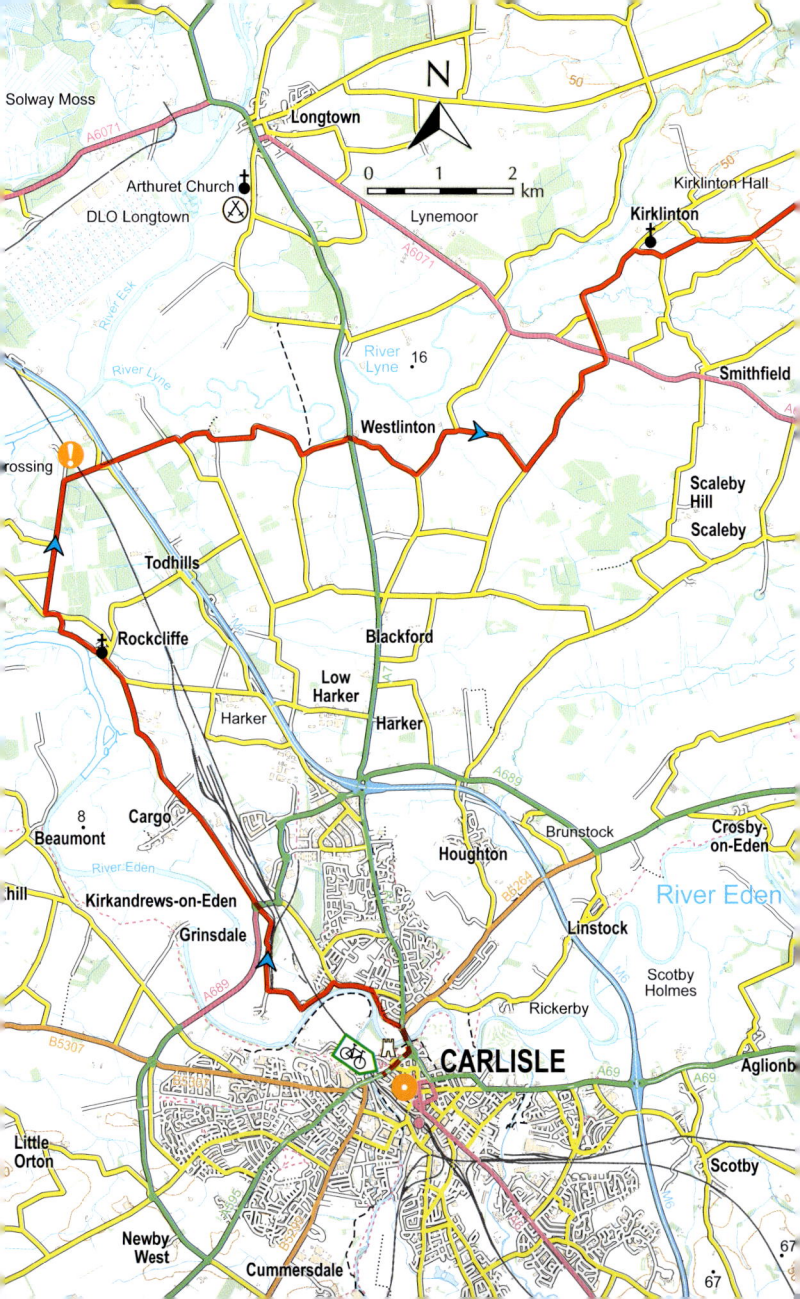

Just after the road bends rightwards away from the Eden, merge left and continue towards Gretna for another 2 miles, through a small forest and **level crossing** to cross a bridge over the M6. Ignore other cycling signage in the area. **Westlinton** is easily reached in under 3 miles. There is little here in the way of amenities, so carefully cross the **A7** as it passes through the village, then continue in the same direction, turning left at the T-junction a mile later.

Fork rightwards to Gill at the next junction, then left at the T-junction 500 metres after the farm. After a further 2 miles of riding into increasingly remote landscapes, cross directly over the **A6071**, then continue to cross Burnside Bridge. The small village and eye-catching church of **Kirklinton** is reached after a further mile.

St Cuthbert's Church at Kirklinton

Day 2 – Carlisle to Bailey Mill

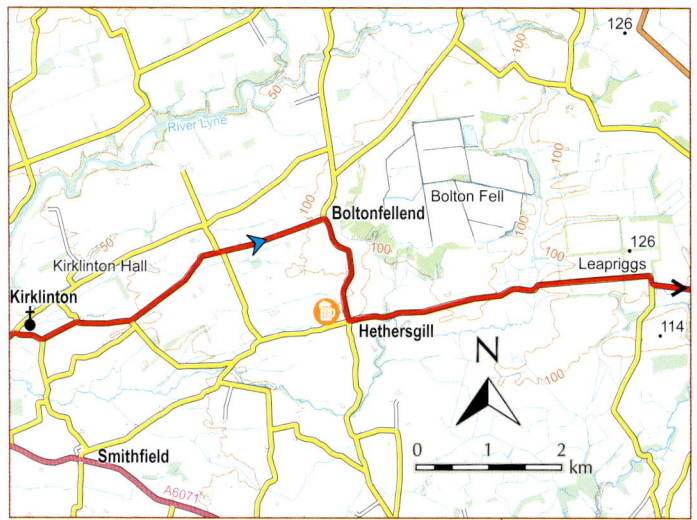

Close to Kirklinton's St Cuthbert's Church is **Kirklinton Hall**, a semi-ruined country house built in 1660 from the stone of an original 12th-century stronghold of Richard de Boyville (ancestor of the Boyle clan). It has since been used by the RAF during World War 2 as well as becoming a nightclub and casino during the swinging 60s.

Head right at the church, then branch left after 400 metres at a junction. Turn right at a T-junction half a mile later, then take the next left. This leads to the hamlet of **Boltonfellend** where a sharp right turn is taken towards Hethersgill. Height is gained almost imperceptibly on this section, with the fells of Kershope Forest becoming visible ahead. On meeting the crossroads in **Hethersgill**, the **Black Lion pub is reached with a right turn**. The Reivers Route, however, requires a left turn uphill then a gradual open climb through **Leapriggs**. The road then makes an obvious right turn; take the first left after this towards Kirkcambeck.

Map continues on page 52

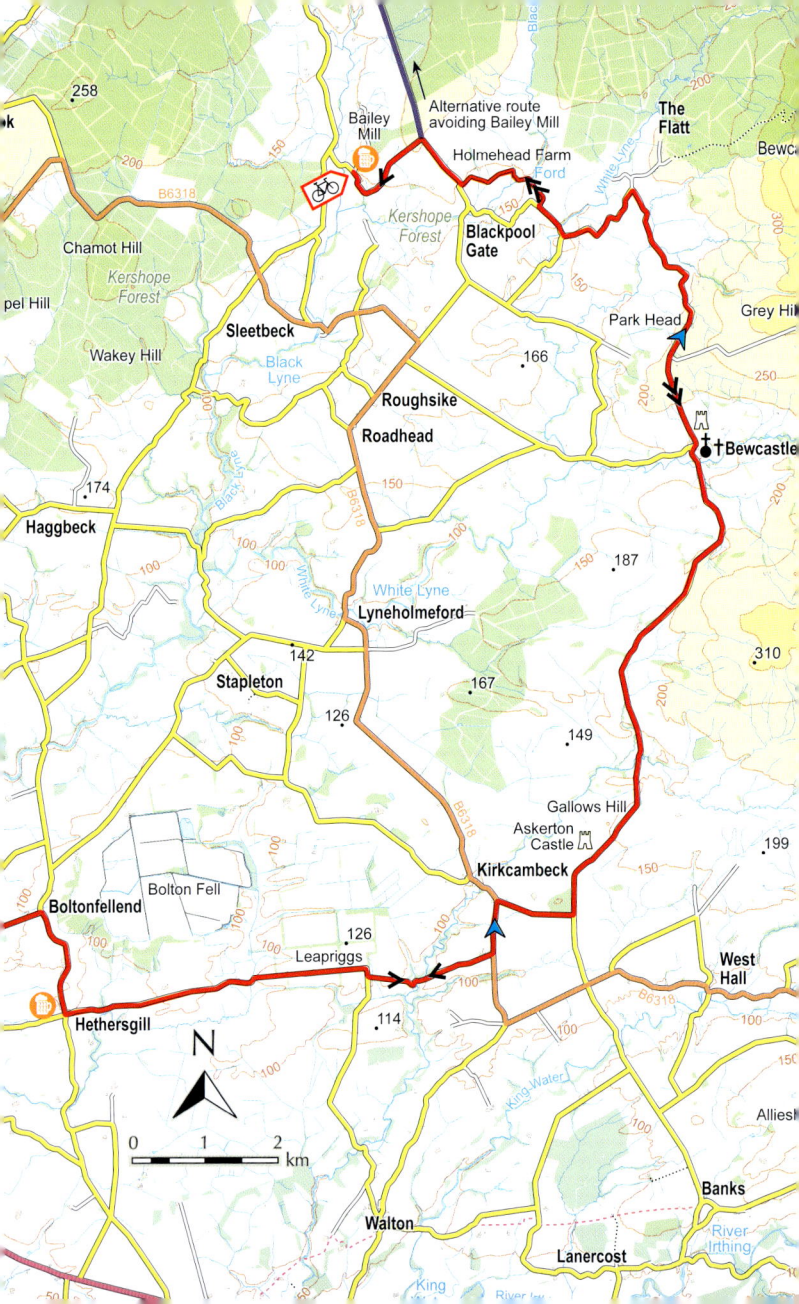

Day 2 – Carlisle to Bailey Mill

Descend to cross a bridge over Cam Beck, then climb again and at the next T-junction turn left onto a wider road. After 400 metres on this, take the first right towards Askerton Castle. The route traverses the wooded slopes of Fell Hill until meeting another T-junction. Here go left towards Bewcastle. Follow the quiet undulating road past the easily missed **Askerton Castle** (on your left behind a barn) and across **Gallows Hill**. ▶

A high and open stretch of 4 miles leads to **Bewcastle**. It is easy to imagine the drama and conflict of the Reivers played out against the wild remote landscape hereabouts.

Fork right after the church to reach the **castle** itself and then brace yourself for the impending and toughest climb of the day over a cattle grid and along an unlikely boulevard of twisted hawthorns.

Go straight on for 3 miles, enjoying expansive views of the Bewcastle fells to your left and some gradual descent. At a T-junction, with no cycling signage as of

The approach to Bewcastle

Askerton Castle was built in the 15th century. It protected the surrounding area from raids by Liddesdale Reivers in particular.

Map continues on page 56

BEWCASTLE

Bewcastle is an essential stop-off point. Behind the 13th-century St Cuthbert's Church, a small museum about the Reivers and Border history is hidden. Both church and museum are open but unmanned from 9am until dusk. The Roman Bewcastle Fort was once an outpost of Hadrian's Wall, built in an unusual hexagonal shape on the pre-existing shrine to the war god Cocidius. Garrisoned by men from Dacia in modern Romania, it was abandoned by the beginning of the fourth century. In the churchyard stands the unmissable 4m shaft of Bewcastle Cross – an eighth-century treasure and one of the best surviving Anglo-Saxon crosses in Britain. The figures and runes depicted are remarkably intact given the cross's exposed situation. The Anglo-Saxon monk St Cuthbert, for whom the church is named, is the patron saint of northern England. His remains passed through Bewcastle when they were moved to prevent them from being destroyed by Viking raiders.

The ornate carvings of Bewcastle Cross

The atmospheric ruins of Bew Castle are just beyond the church. The original castle was a stronghold for wealthy local families, until being raided and finally destroyed in 1321. It then became a Scots manor and later the property of King Edward IV and King Richard III. During the 16th century the castle was garrisoned in an attempt to control the reiving families hereabouts. Reflecting this, a border ballad tells the story of a tenant farmer, 'Jamie Telfer o' the Fair Dodhead', who was reputably raided by the captain of Bewcastle and his troops. However, the historical source of this Reiver ballad is, like many others, limited. The castle fell into disrepair after the Union of the Crowns. Among its interesting features were the 'murder holes' in the walls which were used for pouring boiling liquid down onto enemies.

DAY 2 – CARLISLE TO BAILEY MILL

2020, go left, almost doubling back on yourself. Here, there is a short gentler section before more climbing, with fells and forest panoramas.

After 1½ miles, take another currently unsigned right turn (the first available) to immediately cross the **White Lyne** river on a little-used bridge with white rails. Fork right after 400 metres then follow the tarmac road as it bends left and then dips steeply down hairpins past a 'ford' sign. The descent can be gravelly, but rest assured that the **ford** is an overstatement and easily negotiated. Continue beside the **Black Lyne** for a short distance, then rise again to a junction with a wider road after 500 metres. Turn right and begin a long but steady climb into wilder terrain once again. Near the top of the hill, two Route 10 options present themselves:

- A left turn on the 10 signposted to Bailey Mill is the original and best. The road descends steeply here and quickly loses all the height that has been gained, swooping down towards the huge expanse of Kershope Forest ahead. The lonely hamlet outpost of **Bailey Mill** is soon reached.

- An alternative – also signed 10 – bypasses Bailey Mill by heading straight on (useful for those heading to Newcastleton). This eventually swings westwards to intersect the main route beyond Bailey Mill at Corner

The sign for the oasis of Bailey Mill

Climbing from Kershope Bridge on the road route to Newcastleton

Near Baileyhead on the western alternative road to Kershope Bridge

House, where a beautiful pre-war fingerpost-style cast iron road sign marks Newcastleton 4 miles.

Newcastleton finish

Newcastleton is just over 6 miles further than Bailey Mill and just under 4 miles off the main route. To end the day's riding in Newcastleton, follow the Day 3 route description for 3 miles to **Kershope Bridge** (or take the alternative route from before Bailey Mill straight there), then cross the bridge into Scotland and continue straight ahead to reach the southern end of **Newcastleton**. The onward route is described in the 'On-road alternative via Newcastleton' section in Day 3. If your detour to Newcastleton is purely for an overnight stay, retrace your route to Kershope Bridge to rejoin the main route.

EAST TO WEST

The signage can at times be trickier E–W. Close reading of the text will prove helpful. The steepest climb of the day is short but feisty from the ford near Holmehead Farm – which touches 1 in 4 into its hairpins. Conversely, the climb over to Bewcastle is more gradual than its W–E counterpart. Carlisle is a little trickier in this direction, but is generally still very well signed. The snicket from Etterby Street to Cavendish Terrace is, however, easily missed; it is next to number 73 Etterby Street.

DAY 3
Bailey Mill to Bellingham

Start	Bailey Mill (NY 517 785) or Newcastleton (NY 484 877)
Finish	Bellingham (TQ 374 717)
Distance	37 miles (60km) (it is the same distance from Newcastleton on road)
Total ascent	875m (737m from Newcastleton taking road alternatives)
Steepest climb	After crossing the footbridge beyond Havering Bog at Scotch Knowe in the heart of the Kielder Forest traverse there is a 25m challenge hill that peaks at roughly 2 in 5 on loose aggregate – fun to attempt. There is a fairly stiff 1 in 6 climb on Boggle Hill at Rushend Farm, 6½ miles before Bellingham.
Terrain	Day 3 of the Reivers Route has roughly 20 miles on unsurfaced tracks and paths and 17 miles on minor roads. The Kielder Forest traverse is on tracks: the first half to Scotch Knowe is at times rocky and uneven. After reaching the high point of the Reivers Route (357m) on the forest traverse, the track surface improves, with the last 3½ miles after Willowbog down to the reservoir being smoother and faster. The gravel cycle path around Kielder Water is excellent and makes for superb riding. The initial 400 metres towards Falstone from Kielder Dam is on loose aggregate, then on a muddy and grassy track that also requires care. The on-road alternative via Newcastleton is significantly different.
OS maps	Landranger 79 and 80 or Explorer OL42
Refreshments	Bailey Mill, Leaplish Waterside Park on Kielder Water (water bottles can be filled at the outside tap on 'The Bike Place'), Tower Knowe visitor centre, Falstone. (Also at Hermitage on the B6399 and at Kielder village for the on-road route.)
Intermediate distances	Kershope Bridge 3 miles (5km), Scotch Knowe bridge 10 miles (16km), Lewis Burn bridge 16 miles (26km), Leaplish Waterside Park 19 miles (31km), Tower Knowe visitor centre 23 miles (37km), Falstone 25 miles (40km), Lanehead 30 miles (48km)

In many ways, this day is what truly distinguishes the riding on the Reivers Route from other coast-to-coast routes. Primarily, this is because the day involves a fascinating off-road traverse of Kielder Forest that follows the line of the England–Scotland border for its first 5½ miles and incorporates the high point of the Reivers Route at 357m. Admittedly, its forest tracks are not terrain over which to move quickly, but the whole passage is not particularly demanding and navigation is relatively easy. The first half of the traverse heads upstream and, while over 230m of height is gained, this is achieved at such a gradient as to make the ride appear mostly flat. The second half of the forest traverse heads downstream with an overall descent to the lake of 165m.

The forest traverse evokes a spellbinding sense of remoteness and proves a real cycle-touring highlight to be relished, although the road alternative going via Newcastleton is also good (see 'On-road alternative' description). If undertaking the latter, a short detour is recommended in order to incorporate the bewitching Hermitage Castle – arguably one of the most impressive ruined buildings in Britain. After the remoteness of the forest interior – where the isolated Kershopehead bothy lies 200 metres off route across Kershope Burn – meeting Kielder Water with its tourist infrastructure imparts a sense of returning to civilisation. At Kielder Water a popular waterside track leads satisfyingly to Kielder Dam. Thereafter, another mile of off-road cycling intercedes before minor gated roads lead without complication to Bellingham.

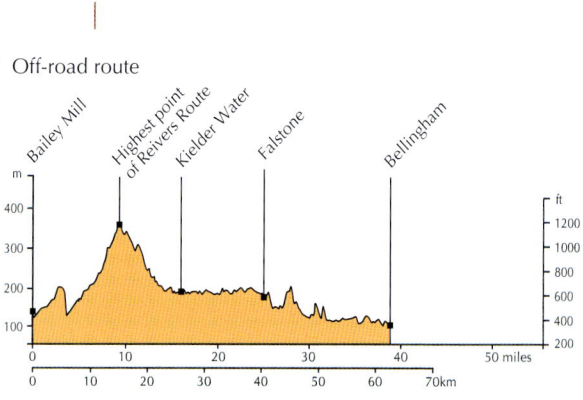

DAY 3 – BAILEY MILL TO BELLINGHAM

On-road alternative route

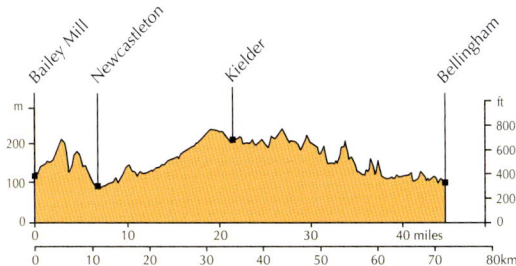

From **Bailey Mill** head downhill to cross Bailey Water and continue to a T-junction. Turn right (10 signage currently missing). Continue for 2½ miles to the junction at **Corner House** just before Roansgreen. Take a left (essentially straight on), then eventually descend hairpin bends to **Kershope Bridge**. ▶ Do not cross the bridge. Instead, take the forest track on the right immediately before it. The Kielder Forest traverse is now underway – a true highlight of the route. (For the on-road alternative route via

Kershope Burn forms part of the 96-mile (155km) England–Scotland border.

Map continues on page 60

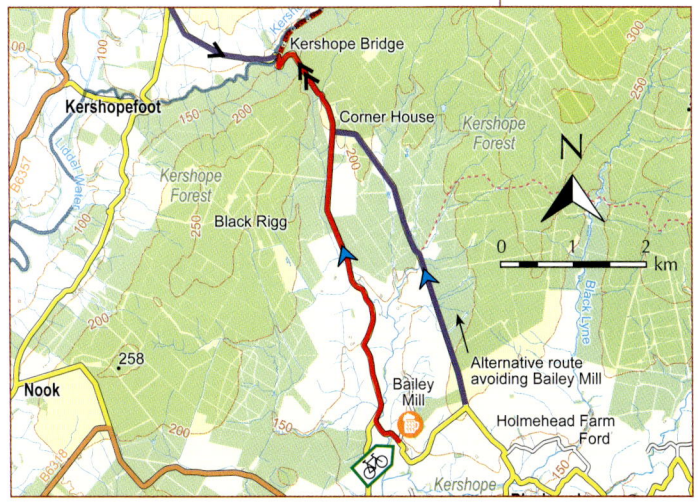

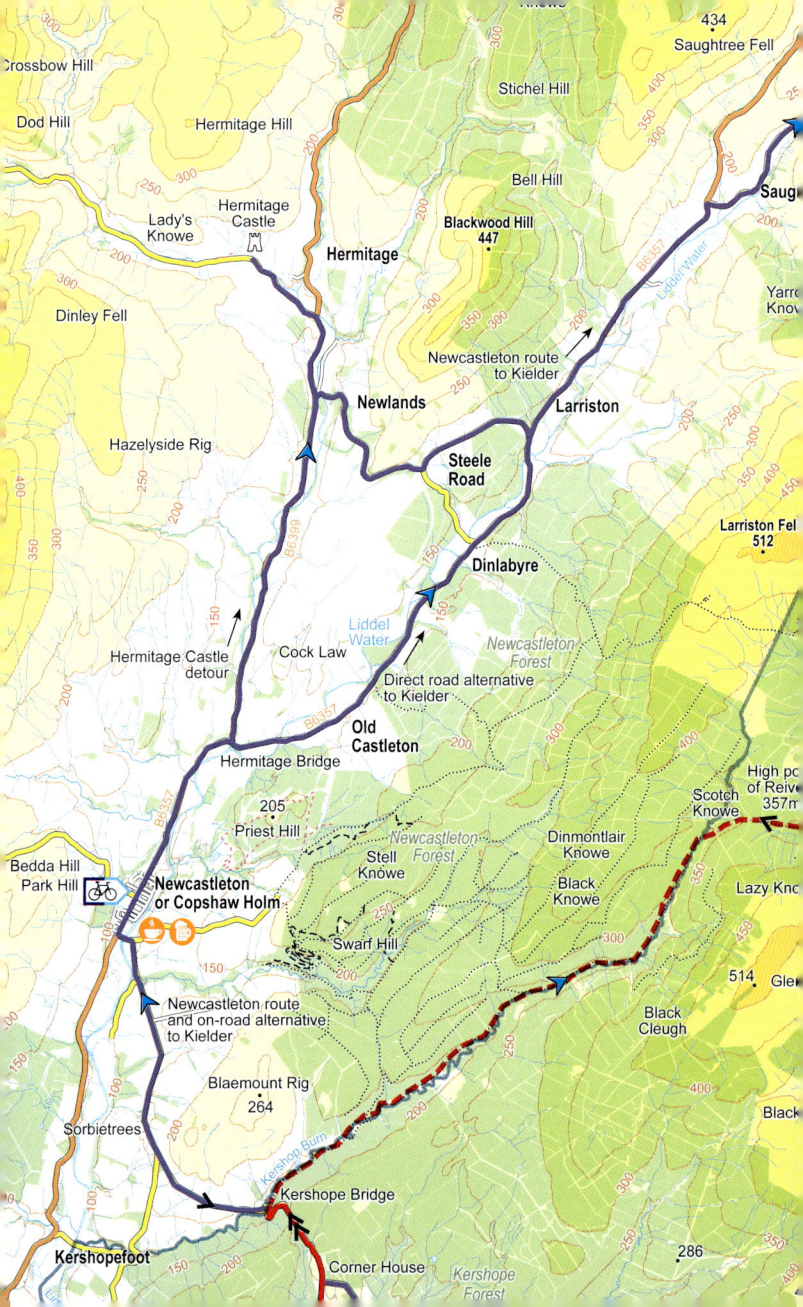

Superb riding beside Kershope Burn

KERSHOPE BRIDGE AND KIELDER FOREST TRAVERSE

The unassuming Kershope area undoubtedly saw considerable Reiver action. Indeed, the border ballad 'Jamie Telfer o' the Fair Dodhead' describes a Reivers skirmish in the vicinity: 'O many a horse ran masterless / The splintered lances flew on high / But o'er they went to the Kershope ford / The Scotts had gotten the victory.' Leaving the bridge on dark or grim weather days for the Kielder Forest traverse can provoke a sense of foreboding as civilisation is left behind – such conditions make the experience all the more invigorating and memorable, especially if solo.

The foreboding is not, perhaps, unfounded. The Davidson Monument stands in a forest clearing half a mile SW of the route and commemorates Thomas Davidson, a local gamekeeper murdered by means of neckerchief strangulation in the forest in 1849 (see Appendix C – Further reading). Likewise, a pillar at Bloody Bush 1½ miles N of the route reputedly marks the site of a brutal England–Scotland border battle; it was later a toll gate. For those who might revel in the sinister aura of these parts, there is a two-storey bothy 200 metres SW of the Reivers Route across the Kershope Burn (no access bridge) at Kershopehead, NY 544 863. The bothy can be reached directly via permissive forest tracks from Kershope Bridge. The forest would also provide a spooky wild camp (use the Scottish side of the border).

Day 3 – Bailey Mill to Bellingham

Newcastleton and Kielder village, see the description at the end of the stage.)

Follow the track along the valley floor. The terrain can be rough and bumpy at times. After a mile, take the left fork crossing a bridge over Kershope Burn into Scotland. Thereafter, follow the track on the immediate left (Scottish side) of the burn, ignoring any branch tracks. After roughly 5½ miles the footbridge beyond Havering Bog at **Scotch Knowe** is reached. ▶

Cross the footbridge – the track becomes narrow here for roughly half a mile. A 50-metre flat section above the bridge allows you to get speed up in order to attempt the impending obvious short ramp. This is audaciously steep near its brow; a gold star if you manage it without a foot down or a bike push – we didn't! After the ramp, a gentle climb is made to the unmarked **high point of the Reivers Route**. Here a wide track is joined for the protracted descent to Kielder Water.

> There is a 'Welcome to Scotland' sign at Scotch Knowe, two picnic benches and, 200 metres downstream, a few pools in the burn suitable for paddling.

Crossing out of Scotland at the bridge over Kershope Burn by Havering Bog

Map continues on page 66

The route passes to the left of the isolated private dwelling at **Willowbog** and climbs fairly steeply to a T-junction with another track that is slightly better surfaced – **Bloody Bush Road**. Turn right and follow this down the valley, at first on the north of Akenshaw Burn but eventually on the south side of Lewis Burn. A purpose-built shared-use reservoir cycle path, 'Lakeside Way', is met at the impressive curved **Lewis Burn suspension bridge**.

Note: At the suspension bridge, a left can be taken over the bridge, where continuing on Lakeside Way will lead without significant climbing to Kielder village in 3–4 miles (pub, campsite, café and bike hire/repair).

Leaplish has a pub-restaurant, shop, café and bicycle hire/repair shop with an out tap for filling water bottles.

To continue on the Reivers Route from Lewis Burn suspension bridge, do not cross the bridge but join Lakeside Way on the left and follow it rightwards under the road bridge and round to the landing at **Matthews Linn** (toilets). Lakeside Way then leads without complication to **Leaplish Waterside Park** in 2 miles. ◄

Day 3 – Bailey Mill to Bellingham

The Reivers Route/Lakeside Way leading out from the slightly disorientating Leaplish Waterside Park is harder to locate than might be expected; it begins on a narrow track on the left above the pub and the shop, but below the level of the bicycle hire shop and just below the exit road. At the first minor hill on the track an 'open door' sculpture lures many for a photo.

A descent eventually leads in half a mile to a sharp direction change at a water inlet. The official Reivers Route cuts out the circuitous **Bull Crag Peninsula** section of the Lakeside Way by branching off rightwards shortly after the inlet. A fairly challenging uphill is followed by a pleasant winding downhill where a signed '10' right turn on the descent leads back onto the Lakeside Way at the Cranecleugh Burn bridge. Conversely, staying with the flatter but considerably longer and more time-consuming Lakeside Way is a viable alternative.

Crossing the threshold of one of the many sculptures on Kielder Water's Lakeside Way near Leaplish

KIELDER WATER

Kielder Water has the greatest water capacity of any man-made reservoir in Britain. The scale of the reservoir, the way it has been carefully harnessed for recreation and the sheer size of the surrounding forest – one of the largest man-made forests in Europe – make it an unusual location in Britain. Opened by the Queen in 1982, only six years after construction began, the reservoir swallowed a section of the long-closed Border Counties Railway line (1858–1958), including the old station at Plashetts, and saw the loss of a collection of farms and a school. Ospreys now swoop over water that rests high above where farmers once trod. Kielder has been designated part of the Dark Sky movement and boasts an observatory which regularly hosts events and talks open to the public. The purpose-built shared cycle and pedestrian Lakeside Way follows the shoreline and is replete with a series of modern sculptures and installations. A circumnavigation of the whole lake on the Lakeside Way is a delight. As of 2020, there is no shop in Kielder village and the YHA has closed down. The campsite has very few supplies – but does have midge nets! Victuals can be purchased at the cosy Anglers Arms in Kielder village and at the Kielder Castle café, while Leaplish Waterside Park has all necessary amenities and a bird of prey centre. A ferry operates in summer.

CYCLING THE REIVERS ROUTE

Tower Knowe has toilets, a café and a small free museum/visitor centre.

Cross the Cranecleugh Burn bridge and continue, briefly running close to but never joining the main road on the way to **Tower Knowe**. ◄ From here the Lakeside Way continues to reach the impressive **Kielder Dam** in just over half a mile. Cross the dam on a road to Hawkhope car park (toilets). From here a switchback ramp leads uphill and eastwards, passing the plaque Queen Elizabeth II unveiled at the reservoir opening in 1982. The tarmac ceases here and a very loose limestone aggregate track **requiring considerable care** is followed downhill from the dam (although this can be avoided by joining the main road at the southern end of the dam and, after a mile, turning left downhill to the T-junction in Falstone close to where the off-road route joins the road).

After 400 metres or so an uphill on the left is ignored in favour of continuing straight on along a soon grassy and muddy track. This merges onto a road and shortly after reaches a T-junction at the northern edge of

DAY 3 – BAILEY MILL TO BELLINGHAM

Falstone – which can be visited by turning right under the old railway bridge. ▶

Falstone has a tearoom/shop and a good pub, the Blackcock Inn.

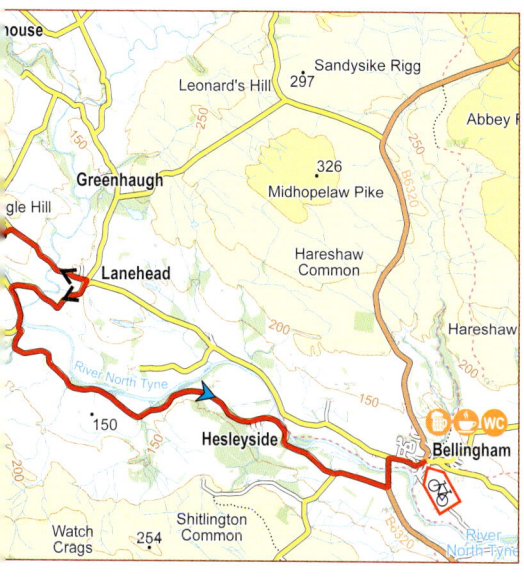

On gated roads near Falstone

At the T-junction in Falstone, turn left and climb gradually along a minor (regularly gated) road allowing great views across the River North Tyne valley where lost Reiver bastle ruins lurk in the woodland or have been incorporated into farm buildings. Eventually, a steady climb leads to the former Thorneyburn train station – now a private house. Here the old railway line is crossed at what still feels like a level crossing – beware the ghost train!

After a gradual descent, a sharp bend to the left commences a surprisingly fierce climb up **Boggle Hill** – the steepest road climb of the day – to pass Rushend Farm. On reaching the T-junction at **Lanehead**, take care turning right to head steeply downhill. The road doubles back to cross first Tarset Bridge and then a bridge over the **River North Tyne**, where an immediate left, signposted to Birks and **Hesleyside**, is taken.

BELLINGHAM

Bellingham – pronounced 'Bellin-jum' – is a pleasant village that functions as a hub for the surrounding areas and a base for the Northumberland National Park. It has an array of amenities, including guest houses, a youth hostel, shops, pubs and cafés (Carriages Tearoom is based in an old train carriage on the NCN 68, 100 metres beyond the second Reivers turning). The village bakery proved a regular fuelling stop for the authors while compiling this book. For those hiking northwards on the Pennine Way, Bellingham has long been the first welcome respite after leaving Hadrian's Wall, which lies 13 miles or so to the south. The village is steeped in history, particularly from Viking times, including an association with St Cuthbert after whom a church in the village takes its name, and through the period of the Border Reivers. The village heritage centre is a good place to learn, among other things, about the legend of 'Lang Pack'. This tells of a man concealed in a long package who attempted a Trojan-horse-style attempt at burglary. His ruse failed and resulted in his death – a long grave in St Cuthbert's churchyard is reputedly his resting place. Bellingham was the territory of the Charltons in reiving times, who at least twice attacked the long-gone Bellingham Castle and fought battles with March Warden Fenwick here.

Day 3 – Bailey Mill to Bellingham

Continue straight on with only one short steepish climb interrupting the flow of pleasant undulating terrain to reach a T-junction with the **B6320**. A left here leads to **Bellingham** in half a mile.

On-road alternative via Newcastleton
This option is very easy to navigate and a worthwhile route in its own right, even more so when the alluring Hermitage Castle is included in the day's itinerary.

From **Kershope Bridge**, ride across Kershope Burn into Scotland, quickly gaining height onto open moorland. A flatter section with great views across Liddesdale leads through the hamlet of **Sorbietrees** (B&B) then descends to cross Tweeden Burn and **Liddel Water**. At the T-junction turn right onto the main road through **Newcastleton**.

LIDDESDALE

Liddesdale may look the picture of tranquillity now, but its appearance belies its former reputation as home to some of the fiercest Border Reivers clans and one of the most dangerous places in Europe. It was presided over by both the Armstrongs and Elliots, who held no truck with either the English or Scots' crowns and lived by the law of clan allegiance. In the heyday of the Reivers, Liddesdale was the scene of numerous bloody raids, battles, murders and reprisals. There were once 70 fortified pele towers in the valley and the Armstrongs alone could command a force of 3000 horsemen. Liddesdale is immortalised in the famous border ballad 'Jock o' the Side' which tells the tale of a failed raid and the daring rescue of reiver Jock Armstrong.

Newcastleton (also known as Copshaw Holm) was founded in 1793 as a result of land clearances where cottagers and tenant farmers were forced off the land in Old Castleton and settled here. The village is a base for the 7stanes mountain biking trails. In 2018, Newcastleton opened its own community-funded unmanned petrol station. The village also has a small museum about the area's history on the main street.

Beside Liddel Water in peaceful northern Liddesdale

Continue through Newcastleton on the B6357. There is some fast traffic on the stretch out of town, but it never seems to get unpleasantly busy. After riding beside Liddel Water for a mile, cross the river on **Hermitage Bridge**. A right turn towards Kielder, immediately after the bridge, can now be taken (although the following route is strongly recommended).

Hermitage Castle route
A superb and almost circular detour to the imposing and unforgettable Hermitage Castle can be made here, adding very little overall distance to the on-road alternative. The castle is 5 miles away from Newcastleton, but by cutting back to the main on-road alternative, incorporating a visit only adds 4¾ miles to the total day's riding. From the bridge, swing left, initially following the eastern bank of Hermitage Water on what is now the **B6399**. The castle is well-signed with a left turn from the B6399 at the Old Hermitage Schoolhouse, now Horn & Country Crafts, which has a little shop selling ice cream, soft drinks and snacks.

DAY 3 – BAILEY MILL TO BELLINGHAM

HERMITAGE CASTLE

The somewhat sinister-looking Hermitage Castle was originally built in the 13th century but was heavily fortified in the 1500s, standing guard as it did over what was once the bloodiest valley in Britain. The castle has connections with Mary Queen of Scots, who is reputed to have ridden 25 miles here for a tryst with her future husband Earl Bothwell after he was wounded by the reiving Elliots. On Mary's return journey, she was thrown by her horse and contracted a fever. The castle has a torrid history of changing hands between the English and Scots; tales of battles, murders and demonic inhabitants abound and the building itself is enough to send shivers down most people's spines. Nearby Hermitage chapel also has bloodthirsty legends associated with it, including that of the unfortunate giant Cout of Kielder and the dark Lord Soules, who met grisly endings here.

From Hermitage, retrace your steps to the B6399, then turn right in the direction of Newcastleton for just over half a mile before turning left (signed to Steele Road) to cross a weak bridge over Hermitage Water. The road climbs over Steele Fell, giving superb views, then begins a descent through a former railway bridge and the

The impressive defences of Hermitage Castle

hamlet of **Steele Road**, and continues to reach the **B6357** Liddesdale road. Turn left here to rejoin the direct Kielder route and continue for 2½ miles to the unmissable right turn signed to Kielder Water at **Saughtree**.

Direct Kielder route

Turn right after Hermitage Bridge and follow the **B6357** road up Liddesdale, crossing Liddel Water on a bridge next to the old stone bridge. Shortly afterwards, the site of **Old Castleton** is passed, with the ancient village's market cross still visible in the field opposite the graveyard. The raised earthworks of the castle which gave the village its name are a little further on to the left.

Having cycled roughly 6½ miles from Hermitage Bridge, take an unmissable right turn signed to Kielder Water. This passes through the hamlet of **Saughtree**, and continues on a wonderful open minor road right beside Liddel Water for about 5 miles of straightforward scenic riding to eventually reach a raft of signage announcing a return into England and Northumberland near **Deadwater**, where there was once a train station. A further 3 miles of uncomplicated riding with more forested areas leads to **Kielder** campsite and village, on the left.

Those on road bikes can carry on along this road, which runs above the south-west side of Kielder Water. However, from this point onwards vehicles have a tendency to drive fast on this purpose-built wide road, which has the feel of an A-road but without the heavy traffic flow. (Alternatively, the Lakeside Way is just about doable – if less than ideal – on a road bike.)

All those on touring, hybrid and gravel bikes will certainly want to join the fantastic Lakeside Way as soon as possible. The simplest way to do this is to carry on for just over half a mile past Kielder village to the next left turn. Take this, turning right after 50 metres onto the Lakeside Way around the south-western side of the lake. After 3 miles, at the impressive Lewis Burn suspension bridge over the mouth of Lewis Burn, the off-road Reivers Route joins the Lakeside Way; continue to **Bellingham** as described earlier in the stage.

St Oswald's Church in Bellingham

EAST TO WEST

The descent to Scotch Knowe from the Reivers Route high point requires considerable caution with 20 metres on a narrow path that feels like a drop. It is steeper than 1 in 3 and most will feel it prudent to dismount, although the run-out is relatively straight for 50 metres. There are testing road climbs, particularly between Bellingham and Falstone. However, the hardest climb of the day involves overcoming the hairpin bends above Kershope Bridge which are followed by a further half-mile of climbing. The trickiest off-road climb is on loose limestone aggregate to reach the top of Kielder Dam. The ascents on the Kielder Forest traverse are more obviously pronounced in this direction, but never brutal. There are no significant route-finding difficulties E–W. Look out for a signed left off the Lakeside Way after the footbridge near Bull Crag if you wish to cut out the Bull Crag Peninsula. Leaplish Waterside Park can be disorientating: the Reivers Route enters above the shop and pub, but below 'The Bike Place'. It then leaves the area just beyond the bicycle hire shop and playground. Alternatively, it can be joined from the road trending north from the bottom of the playground, or another path by the water's edge.

CYCLING THE REIVERS ROUTE

DAY 4
Bellingham to Tynemouth

Start	Bellingham (TQ 374 717)
Finish	Tynemouth (NZ 374 691)
Distance	51 miles (82km)
Total ascent	764m
Steepest climb	Shortly after leaving Bellingham, the 1¼-mile-long climb from Redesmouth Bridge rears up appallingly after the bridge, allowing almost no time to change down gears for a brutal lung-opening 1 in 5. The climb then eases into a more protracted haul up Buteland Fell. The double-humped climb up to Ryal on Fairspring Banks is deceptively steep and far tougher than it looks!
Terrain	On superb quiet roads for the first two-thirds of the day. On the approach to Ponteland there is one section of unmade track which road bikers will want to avoid (see alternative route). Much of the rest of the riding is on well-surfaced disused rail lines and other traffic-free paths in Tyneside, none of which will pose problems for any bikes.
OS maps	Landranger 80, 87 and 88.
Refreshments	Matfen, Stamfordham, Ponteland and numerous spots thereafter
Intermediate distances	Birtley 6 miles (10km), Thockrington 12 miles (19km), Ryal 21 miles (34km), Matfen 24 miles (39km), Stamfordham 27 miles (43km), Ponteland 33 miles (53km), Seaton Burn 38 miles (61km), Backworth 43 miles (69km)

This is a day of two halves. The first is a delightful continuation of the hilly Northumbrian terrain as the route climbs out of Bellingham and traverses Pennine landscapes on deserted gated roads to Colt Crag, before trending southwards to the bucolic village of Matfen. This spectacular and high remote section is a real highlight of the Reivers Route. The second half of the day from Maften sees the hills melt away to leave pleasant but less memorable rural lanes and villages before heading into the more densely populated

Day 4 – Bellingham to Tynemouth

environs of Ponteland, where the route takes to former railway paths for long periods through the widespread conurbations of North Tyneside. This is a stretch where the Reivers Route has seen many changes over the years, most recently in 2020. Old signage is not always removed. This can be confusing and careful reading of this guide – particularly between Burradon and Backworth – is recommended in order to avoid getting lost. The final leg into Tynemouth takes mainly traffic-free paths to an impressive coastal finish at Tynemouth Castle and Priory.

From the main street in **Bellingham**, turn right after the post office on a road signed to Redesmouth. Fork right shortly after a motor garage to leave town, again following signs to **Redesmouth**.

> The **murderous history of Redesdale** is immortalised in the famous border ballad 'The Death of Parcy Reed'. Reed was Laird of Troughend and

On the protracted climb from Redesmouth

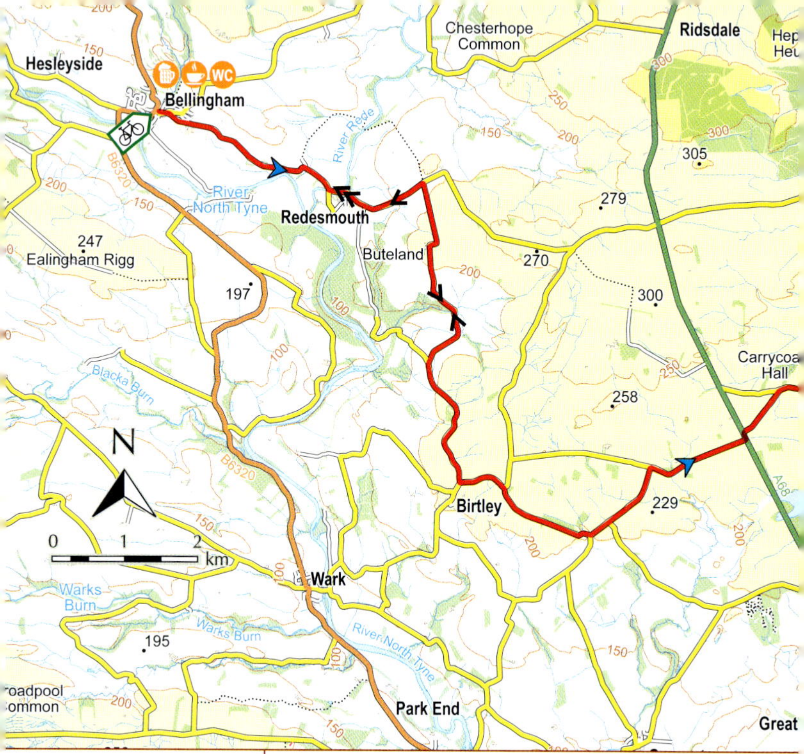

Map continues on page 79

Keeper of Redesdale. He met a bloody fate at the hands of the reiving Croziers. The ballad begins: 'God send the land deliverance/Frae every reaving, riding Scot.'

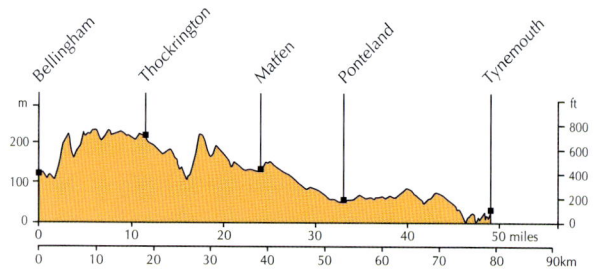

DAY 4 – BELLINGHAM TO TYNEMOUTH

Cross the bridge over the **River Rede**, where a feisty 1 in 5 hill appears as if out of nowhere. The gradient soon eases into a protracted 1¼ mile up the side of Buteland Fell. At the brow of the ominous straight ramp (not as bad as it looks) turn right to pass through the hamlet of **Buteland**.

From Buteland the road descends steeply and care is needed to control speed on its gravelly surface. A gate is met at the crossing of Blackbog Burn. Continue on undulating and infrequently travelled charming terrain to meet a T-junction with a slightly wider road. Turn left here towards Woodburn. Stay straight on this road across high open pasture to emerge at the **A68**. ▶

Do not go onto the A68, but take a left onto a gravel path just before it. This leads in 50 metres to a safe crossing of the A68 onto a minor road signed to Thockrington. Follow this to a junction near the historic seat of the reiving Shafto family at **Carrycoats Hall**, where a 16th-century bastle has been incorporated into the building.

Merge right then soon fork right again towards Thockrington. As of 2020, grass threatened to engulf the narrow tarmac here and the pretty **Colt Crag Reservoir** peeps up from behind the trees ahead. Cross the potholed gravelly bridge over the end of the reservoir, and soon after turn left for a super passage to reach **Thockrington** and its picturesque church.

The A68 follows the course of the Roman road called Dere Street.

Gated roads lead to St Aidan's Church at Thockrington

THOCKRINGTON

Thockrington is now little more than a church and a farm. Once a village stood here, but it was burnt to the ground after becoming infected with the plague by a sailor returning from overseas. The imposing St Aidan's church is one of the oldest in Northumbria. Its graveyard bears testimony to local reiving families such as the Armstrongs, Shaftos and Milburns. Also buried here is Constance Leathart, who in 1927 became the first British female pilot to be granted a licence outside of London. This pioneering aviator, businesswoman, farmer and aero-racer's grave is simply marked with a headstone reading CRL. Thockrington is a lonely and atmospheric place to pause and draw breath.

Map continues on page 80

Shapely escarpments of the **Whin Sill** are particularly visible around here as small crags and bluffs running east to west across the high land. The Sill was formed by magma from tectonic shift nearly 300 million years ago. The Whin Sill west of here also provides a natural defence and vantage point on which a scenic section of Hadrian's Wall is situated. Holy Island Castle is also perched atop the easternmost part of the Sill.

Continue for a final undulating 1km to reach a T-junction with the **B6342**. Here turn left towards Kirkharle for 1km, then take a right turn signed to Hallington.

What at first glance appears to be a bastle on the hillock opposite is actually an 'eyecatcher' **folly**, built in the late 18th century, called Dovecote (and possibly used as one).

There's been a mill on this site since the mid-1600s, when it was first owned by Henry VIII's poultry keeper.

Stay on the same road, which gently rises and falls, to reach a crossroads with a war memorial near **Hallington Mill**. ◄ Turn left at the crossroads towards Ryal, up the challenging double-humped hillside of Fairspring Banks. At the top of the hill is **Ryal**, an attractive hamlet with a **church** dating from the 12th century. There's also a World War 2 pillbox on the left side of the hamlet.

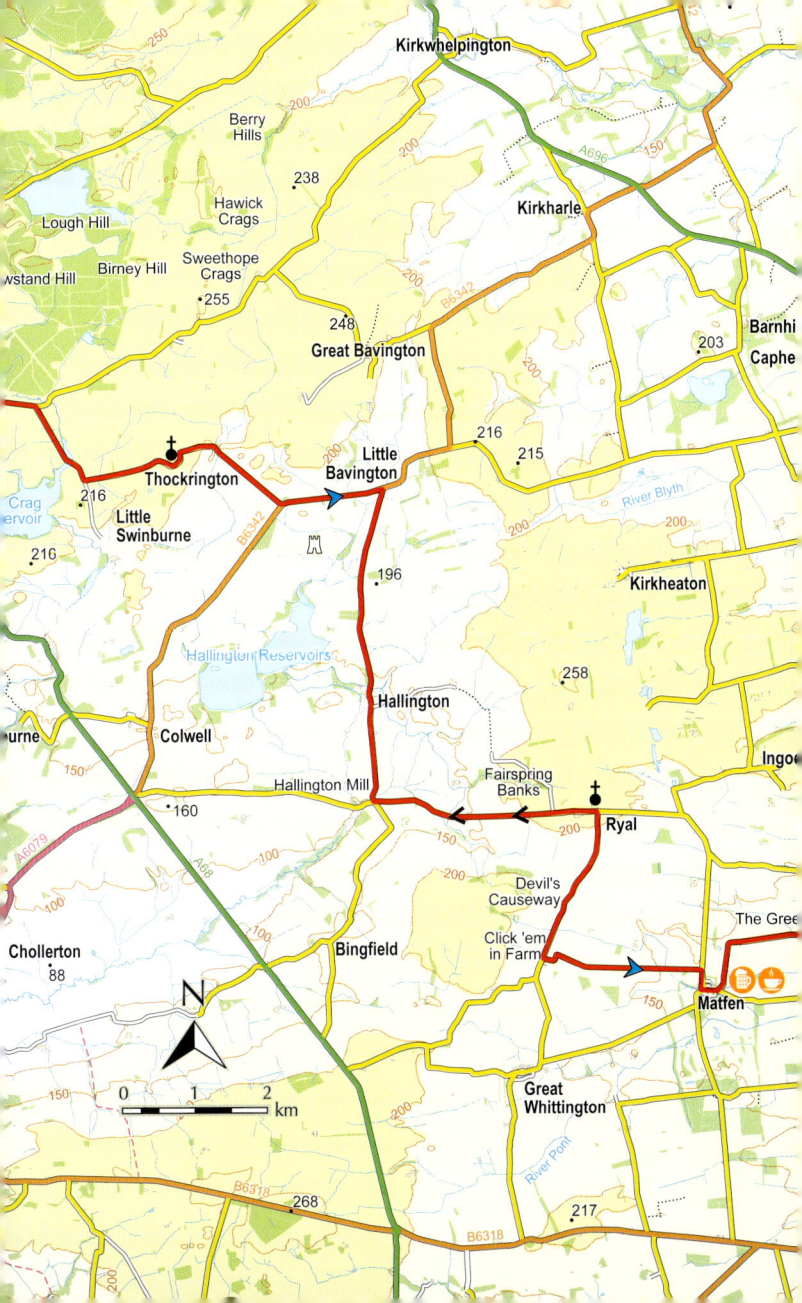

Turn right at the church and swoop down to join the course of the **Devil's Causeway** Roman road for a short distance.

The **Devil's Causeway** runs from Chesters Fort to Berwick-upon-Tweed but predates Hadrian's Wall. The causeway was unusual in that it is thought to have been built solely for cavalry use, rather than marching legions.

The road climbs again through more distinctly rural scenery to the curiously named **Click 'em in Farm**. Just before the farm turn left on a little-used road for 2km of easy riding to a T-junction, where a right turn is taken into the scenic village of **Matfen**. Turn left on the main street beside a village green and stream (signed to Stamfordham). ◄

Matfen has a village shop, lovely tearoom and pub.

From here on in, the scenery feels much less remote and the terrain gradually flattens. The 3km to the next smaller village of **Fenwick** flies by and the way

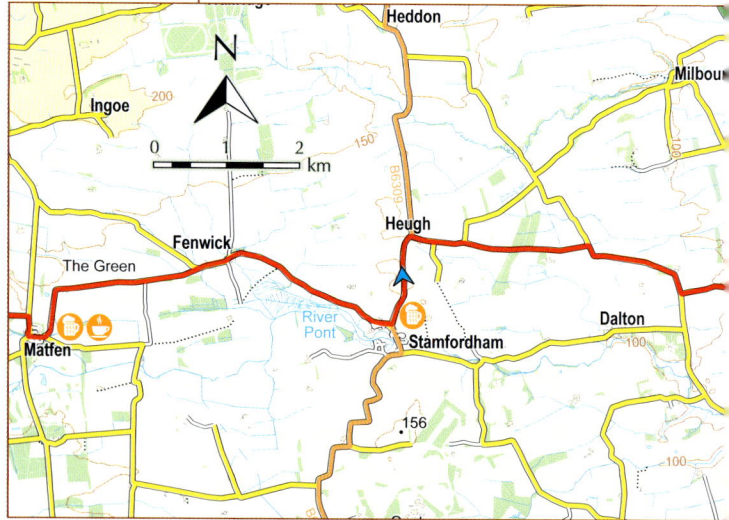

Day 4 – Bellingham to Tynemouth

continues straight ahead to **Stamfordham**, which is just as quickly reached. ▶

Fork left at the end of the main village green, passing the historic village lock-up, then immediately go left uphill on the **B6309**. At the next hamlet of **Heugh**, turn right, passing the easily discernible earthworks of a medieval village on the right. After a mile of flat farmland, go through a wooded area to eventually reach a T-junction, where the route turns right towards Ponteland.

After a further mile of similar terrain, a left turn on Limestone Lane (towards Ponteland again) is taken. After just over a mile, keep your eyes peeled for an easy-to-miss right turn onto a track through fields (if you reach a wooded area on the main road you've gone too far). The track is reasonably surfaced but can become more difficult after rain (an on-road alternative continues to turn right onto the A-road into Ponteland). The track joins the course of a former railway cutting and emerges among the suburbs of **Ponteland** at The Crescent. Care is now needed with route finding.

Stamfordham has a market cross and a village lock-up on its greens. It also has a pub with a small village shop behind it.

Stamfordham is a pleasant place to stop

Map continues on page 85

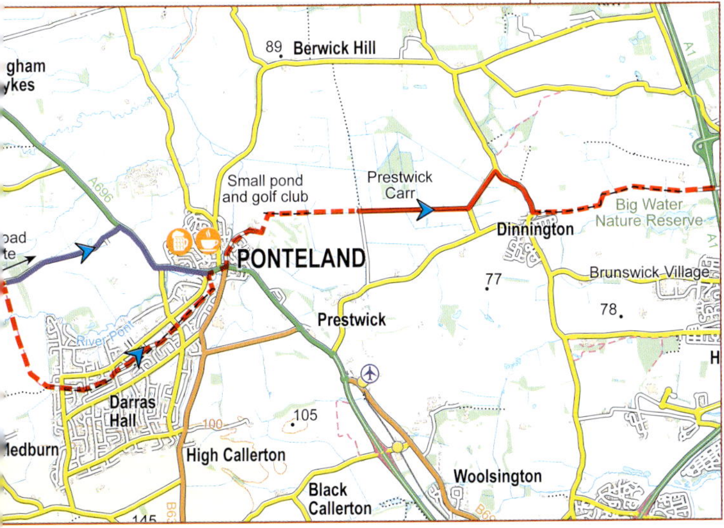

Cycling the Reivers Route

Turn right on Western Way and after only 30 metres go off-road again on a railway path with a small blue cycling sign. This narrow path continues, crossing a minor road by a convenience store and doglegging slightly left down the left side of Ponteland United Reformed Church on Old Station Court cul-de-sac. The path then continues for a further 1km, crossing one further minor road (Eastern Way) where there are metal vehicle barriers which are tricky to negotiate with heavily loaded bikes. Where the path splits at the park, take the right-hand option to meet the **B6323** Callerton Lane, which feels remarkably busy in comparison with most of the Reivers Route.

Turn left on Callerton Lane to reach a junction with the busy **A696**. ◄ Go straight on across this at the traffic lights onto a – thankfully – much quieter stretch of road which follows the River Pont out of town through Elland Hall Farm, with its pond, and past Ponteland's golf course. Stay straight ahead on a badly surfaced road so insanely bumpy it feels like you're riding over ski-slope moguls; the military ranges of **Prestwick Carr** are to your left. Turn left where this bumpy road ends, then right after 400 metres onto a more well-used road.

The road alternative rejoins here.

Just as you enter the village of **Dinnington**, look out for an easily missed left turn onto a dead-end road with cycling signage just after the village 'Welcome' sign. This leads onto a well-made cycle path which crosses farmland to reach a bridge over the **A1**. The route now joins a network of traffic-free paths called the Waggonways which can be somewhat confusing and lacking in clear signage.

> The **North Tyneside Waggonways** are a network of shared-use paths taking the lines of former colliery railways. The coal wagons would originally have been pulled by horses, and then rope-pulled steam haulage and latterly steam locomotives were used on the lines. As well as pits at Seaton Burn and Wideopen, the Waggonways moved coal from more northerly collieries to the River Tyne, where it would be shipped onwards.

About 150 metres after the A1 bridge, take a cycle path left to Seaton Burn. This passes through a housing estate on shared-use paths, crossing Bridge Street in town (amenities), then continuing on the Waggonway path skirting round **Wideopen** to cross Seaton Burn itself into an open area designated as **Weetslade Country Park**. Here there is little signage. Continue heading due east and avoid turn-offs to the left, staying on the main path which becomes two adjacent tracks with higher ground to your left.

Weetslade Country Park is on the site of the old Weetslade Colliery Pit, the former spoil heaps of which comprise the hillocks to the left of the route. The reclaimed site was opened by north-eastern naturalist David Bellamy in 2006.

Keep right at the next fork (do not go uphill) to shortly emerge at a car park. Cross a small road and continue on the Waggonway under the A189, over a rail line and on into **Burradon** – which can be confusing. The standard

The Waggonways navigate through the urban areas at the end of the route

NAVIGATING THE BURRADON/BACKWORTH AREA

Route confusion has arisen in the Burradon/Backworth area and Sustrans has made several sets of changes to the route and its signage. The original route included the nearby bastle of Burradon Tower, whereas another version cut the tower out in favour of heading straight on to pass a small lake. Yet another signed version bypassed the lake on a narrow path. All these itineraries eventually met on the narrow shared-use path beside the B1322 to head into Backworth. None of the options completely succeeded in avoiding a short stretch on or beside a busy road. Unfortunately, signage for the previous courses of the route has not in all instances been removed, while signage was incomplete as of 2020 for the latest course! To add to the muddle, two different Route 10s are marked on the current OS 1:25,000 mapping for this area. Further confusion has arisen with extra unofficial (not blue National Cycle Network) 'Reivers Routes' badging having been added in yet more different places. If you feel you have lost the route entirely, the best course of action is to follow road signs to Backworth, from where the route is easily rejoined.

route crosses the main B-road and continues straight ahead on a cycle path, weaving through a residential area via some ginnels beside houses, into another open area where route finding again needs care.

Variant to Burradon Tower

To visit the 16th-century Burradon Tower, which is on the original route, turn left on the main B-road in Burradon. In 450 metres this bends sharply right; 200 metres later as the road begins to bend back sharply left, turn right – essentially straight on – to Burradon Farm Cottages. Burradon Tower is opposite the cottages. Turn right and head up the track opposite the cottages, until a left can be taken on a Waggonways-signed track. Follow this, bearing left under the **A19** to emerge on Backworth Lane. Turn right on this, using the shared-use narrow pavement to reach **Backworth**.

The 2020 official route joins Backworth Lane from the right at the recreation ground.

DAY 4 – BELLINGHAM TO TYNEMOUTH

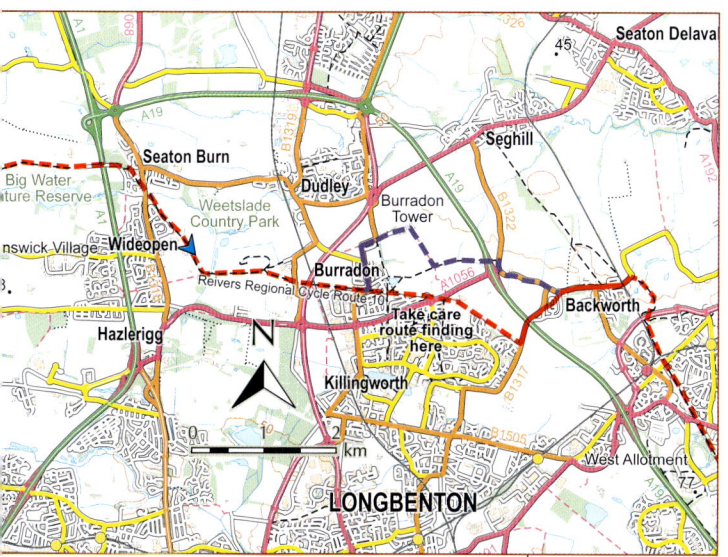

For the current main route from Burradon, fork right at the open area, keeping the back of the housing estate on your right-hand side to emerge on a shared-use pavement beside Green Hills. This skirts the housing and goes left around the side of a roundabout. Almost immediately use a lighted crossing over the **A1056**. After 50 metres beside the road, the path veers away rightwards and becomes Killingworth Waggonway. Ignore the hard right bridleway and continue on the rightwards Waggonway to its end at a T-junction with the **B1317**.

Map continues on page 87

> **Killingworth Waggonway** gave railway pioneer George Stephenson vital experience in rail development. After locomotive trials here, he designed the standard line gauge which is still used in most of the world today.

Turn left on an often unpleasantly busy route into Backworth. This takes a flyover across the **A19**, at the far side of which a huge new housing estate has been built during the writing of this book. It is the authors' understanding that this section is to be routed onto shared-use path. Just after the roundabout for the new housing, the route turns right off the B-road onto Killingworth Lane, to descend through a park on shared-use path, turning right on the main street at the bottom. If this cut-through (which was unsigned at the time of writing) is missed, the same point is reached by continuing down the B-road to a T-junction and making an awkward right turn into the village.

After 600 metres on the main street in **Backworth** the road forks at a mini-roundabout. Take the left option past the church, heading towards Shiremoor and Tynemouth. At a bend just after a level crossing, look out for a right turn with similar signage. This road is soon barred to vehicles and continues on a good bridleway track through an open area.

Stay right where the track forks and go right again on reaching the wooded area which bounds the A186. The track dips under the A-road and then carries on straight as an arrow on Cramlington Waggonway, initially beside a rail line. This track negotiates the built-up area of **Shiremoor** with ease and yields around 4km of pleasant riding, with good crossings at all the roads it intersects.

> The **Stephenson Steam Railway** is located near where the path intersects Middle Engine Lane. A small museum celebrates Tyneside's locomotive heritage and offers short steam-train rides. George and Robert Stephenson spent 20 years in this area developing their pioneering rail work.

The path then runs alongside the North Tyneside Steam Railway line for 2km before entering a more industrial section, still on the traffic-free path. Just after crossing under the A193, the route merges with the 72 C2C route which shares the final few kilometres into Tynemouth with the Reivers. Continue on this and, as the River Tyne draws closer, follow blue signage for Tynemouth on the

DAY 4 – BELLINGHAM TO TYNEMOUTH

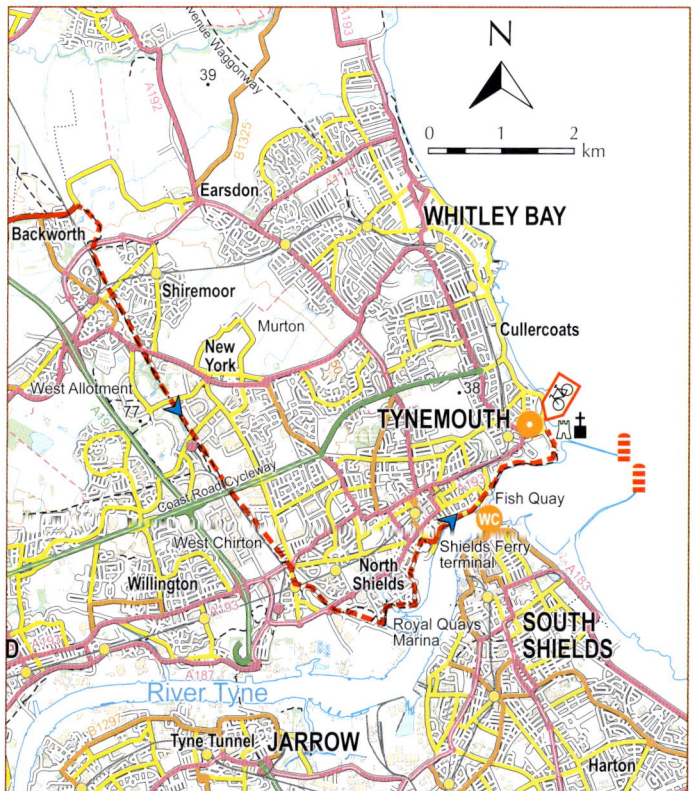

cycle path down the side of a medical centre, dipping under another big flyover and round a leisure centre before snaking downhill to the docks.

The path turns sharply left at the **Royal Quays Marina**, goes along the water's edge for 200 metres, then right across a small bridge. Continue around the harbourside, past hundreds of sailing boats, to join a roadside cycle path up a short hill. At the top, the left onto Dock Road will be unnecessary when the Smith Dock development is completed. If the road through is not open, fork

Cycling the Reivers Route

left onto Dock Road, then immediately right. Escape the estate at a T-junction with a left and immediate right onto Addison Street. This street is a dead end for vehicles, but not to cyclists.

Turn right downhill on Borough Road. At the bottom go left (a hidden right turn leads to the **Shields Ferry terminal** to South Shields and the end of Hadrian's Cycleway). Follow the road, passing new quayside housing developments, to reach **Fish Quay** and a more open section of riverside. ◄

Fish Quay is the biggest prawn port in England.

Just after the white tower of the Fish Quay Low Light house (small museum with fee), turn right onto the quayside path, passing Clifford's Fort and soon reaching the sculpture of three giant-sized buoys commemorating NCN 72 and Reivers Route 10 by a car park and public toilets. The harbourside path is then followed for the remainder of the route.

On this part of the route you will see a large statue of **Lord Cuthbert Collingwood**, who was Admiral Nelson's second in command at the Battle of Trafalgar.

The giant buoy marking the Reivers Cycle Route

Late finish at the end of the ride below the Spanish Battery

▶ The landmark of Tynemouth's Spanish Battery, which probably takes its name from Spanish mercenaries who defended Henry VIII's fleet from gun placements here, looms large and the open North Sea beckons beyond the river's mouth.

Where the promenade ends, the path veers steeply up to a small finger-sign officially marking the route's end and overlooking the bay. Most will want to continue along the headlands to finish at the impressive **Tynemouth Castle and Priory**. For those itching to dip their feet into the North Sea, it is best to lock bikes near the castle and walk down to the dramatic sweep of King Edward's Bay, just below the castle headlands to the north. It is also possible to continue along the path beneath the castle onto the pier to reach the **lighthouse**.

> **Tynemouth Castle** stands proud upon a rocky headland. The castle boasts an impressive moat and ruined gatehouse and keep. The site also combines the ruins of a Benedictine priory, where two kings of Northumbria and one king of Scotland were buried. The site is thought to have been occupied since the Iron Age. The castle is now managed by English Heritage (fee to enter). Tynemouth is nearby and has a wide range of amenities.

The treacherous Black Middens rocks, which wrecked five ships during three days of storms in 1864, lurk in the Tyne beside the route.

Tynemouth Castle is a welcome sight at the route's end

BICYCLES ON THE METRO

Between 10am and 3pm, and after 7pm, bikes are now tolerated on the Metro rail network on certain routes. It is possible to take a bike on the Metro at Tynemouth most of the way into Newcastle (officially cyclists are not meant to get off at Newcastle Central Station but the authors have done this after 7pm without trouble). Otherwise, disembark at Gateshead Stadium and cycle across the river to Newcastle Central Station for onward train journeys: St James Road north, left on the A184 cycle path for 300 metres, right down Albany Road signed 'Gateshead Quays', left on Quayside Road, straight on to Mill Road, left past the Baltic Centre to Millennium Bridge – follow signs to the station thereafter.

EAST TO WEST

Tynemouth to Ponteland is a flat and predominantly traffic-free start to the day but the navigation issues detailed in the stage's main description are equally problematic in this direction. From Ponteland to Stamfordham the population density decreases and the roads become quiet with undulating terrain. From thereon in, the North Pennines rear their heads and there are notable climbs from Matfen to Ryal, up to Hallington and Thockrington, after crossing the A68 towards Birtley and up the south side of Buteland Fell.

THE BORDERERS RIDE
Gretna to Berwick-upon-Tweed

Start	Gretna (NY 316 660)
Finish	Berwick-upon-Tweed (NU 009 524)
Distance	150 miles (241km)
Total ascent	3081m
Steepest climb	A short bike push will almost certainly be necessary to overcome a very short, but very steep 1 in 4 during the off-road section by Ilderton.
Time	3–4 days (the Borderers Ride is of similar difficulty to the main Reivers Route but, having less overall mileage and total ascent, it is equally suited to a three-day challenge or easier four-day ride).
Terrain	To Bellingham, see the Reivers Route. Onwards to Wooler there are several time-consuming off-road sections. The 700-metre section by Ilderton is steep, rocky, muddy and should be treated with caution – as should the road alternative to this, which takes in a relatively busy A-road. Holy Island causeway is tarmacked with a smattering of sand and saltwater to negotiate. The rest of the route to Berwick is mainly off-road and not passable on road bikes; it includes 3km on unmade paths across dunes at Goswick and two shorter muddy clifftop sections to the outskirts of Berwick. A road alternative to these is described.
OS maps	Landranger 85, 86, 79, 80, 74 and 75
Intermediate distances	Bailey Mill 35 miles (56km), Bellingham 60 miles, (97km), Wooler 111 miles (179km)

The Borderers Ride, running coast-to-coast from Gretna to Berwick-upon-Tweed, links the most impressive section of the main Reivers Route with existing parts of the National Cycle Network. It is highly recommended as an alternative itinerary. Designed by the authors, the ride offers cyclists the opportunity to make a more logical and thorough exploration of Border country in the shorter distance of 150 miles. Other Sustrans coast-to-coast routes such as the C2C and Hadrian's Cycleway pass through Whitehaven and use Tyneside as an end point. In contrast, while there are no particular Reivers associations in those areas, the start and finish of the Borderers Ride are the two most famous western and eastern Border towns and give the pleasing symmetry of starting in Scotland and ending in England. The ride heads through the Debateable Lands and follows the England–Scotland border north-eastwards via Holy Island to Berwick. This route provides an even deeper impression of not only the Reivers but of the centuries of bloody Border conflict. Today, cycling through these borderlands gives a real sense of context for modern Britain and the contemporary Scottish Independence debate.

The official start point is beside the Lochmaben Stone, an erratic long-associated with Reiver history and bloody Anglo-Scottish conflicts, on the coast where the River Esk and River Sark empty into the Solway Firth. The ride then passes the renowned elopement destination of the 'Famous' Blacksmiths Shop in Gretna Green and the battlefield of Solway Moss before joining the Reivers Route near Westlinton. At Bellingham, the Borderers Ride diverges from the Reivers Route again, eschewing Tyneside to follow NCN Route 68 to Wooler, taking in far more of the Northumberland National Park and the Cheviots and, with them, some superb reiving sites such as Woodhouse Bastle and Elsdon and Harbottle castles.

From Wooler the ride gains the coast and joins NCN Route 1 (the Coast and Castles South ride), reaching a fitting climax in the dramatic causeway crossing to the Holy Island of Lindisfarne (which is dependent on tide times) and a wild and memorable clifftop entrance to the fascinating town of Berwick, with its long history of border strife and lore.

Day 1: Gretna to Bailey Mill
Start: Gretna (NY 316 660), **Finish:** Bailey Mill (NY 517 785), **Distance:** 35 miles (56km), **Ascent:** 640m

The Borderers Ride starts on the 'coast' south of Gretna at the bleak tidal sands of the Solway Firth. To get there by bicycle from Gretna Green rail station, follow NCN 7 cycling signage. Access the NCN 7 cycle path by steps off the ramp on the north side of the train line. Turn left on the cycle path, passing through tunnels under the railway and A75. After crossing a field for 250 metres the route emerges on a cul-de-sac. The pavement is shared-use. At

THE BORDERERS RIDE – GRETNA TO BERWICK-UPON-TWEED

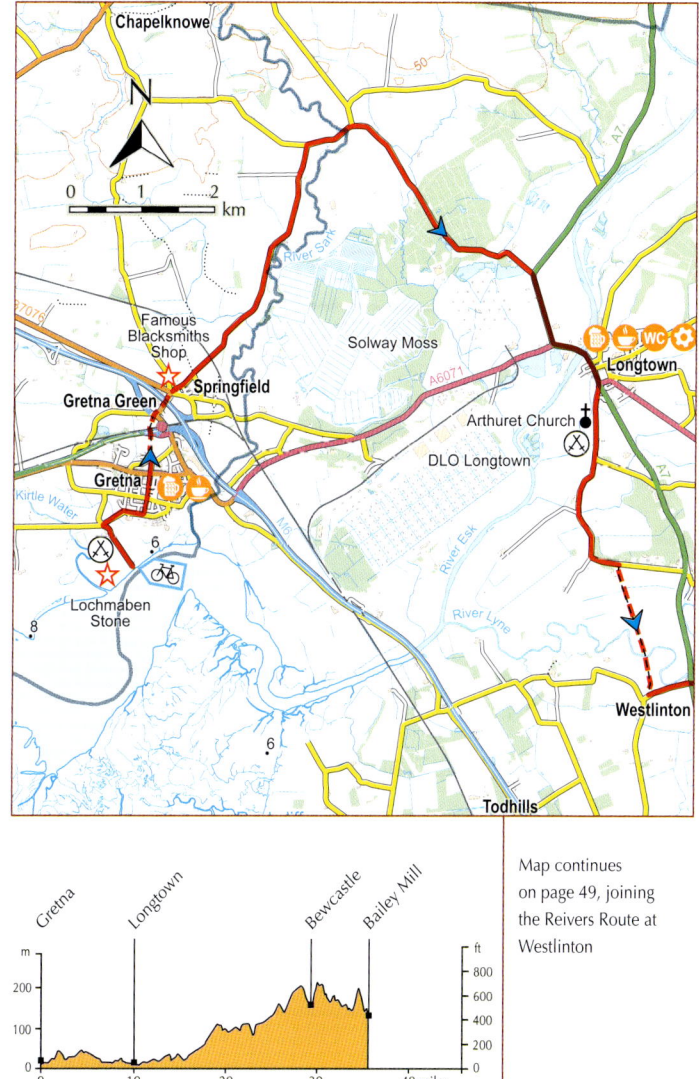

Map continues on page 49, joining the Reivers Route at Westlinton

the T-junction, dogleg left then right almost immediately. At the next crossroads, cross the B721 and carry on more or less straight ahead just to the right of the playground along Central Avenue (this point is easily reached for those arriving by car). Turn right at the next T-junction and in 650 metres at a crossroads turn left off the NCN 7 to pass a farm. Follow this dead-end road to a small parking area at a beach.

From the parking area, reverse the approach route from **Gretna Green station** described previously, joining

THE START OF THE BORDERERS ROUTE

The Lochmaben Stone marked the southernmost limit of the Scottish realm

This point has been chosen as the coastal start of the Borderers Ride due to its historical significance in English–Scottish relations. Some 500 metres to the north of the parking area is the Lochmaben Stone. This gritstone glacial erratic is a 5000-year-old megalith which formed part of a stone circle. Although underwhelming when reached unofficially by 500 metres of very muddy, eroded and difficult-to-follow coastal path (it is on the right in a fenced field), the 2.3m Lochmaben Stone was a key landmark. It marked the southernmost limit of the Scottish realm: meetings, exchanges of prisoners, and assemblies of forces took place here for centuries prior to the Union. The stone is even one of several claiming to be that from which King Arthur reputedly pulled Excalibur! The Battle of Sark, also known as the Battle of Lochmaben Stone, took place in a field north of here in 1448, where the Scots recorded an important victory, with around 3000 English casualties, either killed in battle or drowned.

NCN Route 7. Continue following the well-signed 7 northwards past the train station access steps and making use of the shared-use pavement for most of the way to reach the renowned **Blacksmiths Shop** at the crossroads. Go straight across, following the signs to Corries Mill.

Lovers' hands at the Blacksmiths Shop in Gretna Green

The 'Famous' **Blacksmiths Shop** in Gretna Green now makes the most of its history from 1754 when it became a destination for runaway lovers wishing to take advantage of Scotland's more favourable marriage laws. Today it is a complex of gift shops, café, modern wedding venues and sculptures. The anvil which reputably a blacksmith would have struck to seal a marriage can be found at the centre of an amusing courtship maze. A museum tells the stories of some of the more colourful eloping couples who journeyed to 'the Anvil Priest' at Gretna.

After a brief stop for refreshments, or even nuptials, continue straight ahead past the Blacksmiths complex and out of town into the Debateable Lands, with the soggy plains and peatworks of Solway Moss to the right.

The **Debateable Lands** were a considerable tract of borderland adjoining the northwest bank of the Esk that for over 300 years managed to exist outside of the control of either the English or Scottish crowns. In effect, the area was a de facto independent province. It was 'governed' – in the very loosest sense of the word – by the dominant Reiving clans of the vicinity (most notably the Armstrongs, although others clans held varying degrees of power). The division of the Debateable Lands between the English and Scottish crowns in 1552 redefined the border and proved a key moment in the deconstruction of the Reivers' power.

The next 3 miles of route follow the Scottish side of the **River Sark**, which today forms part of the English-Scottish border. At a T-junction, turn right towards

The coastal start where the Esk empties into the Solway Firth by the Lochmaben Stone

Longtown, which has signed public toilets just off route, is the last guaranteed place to get supplies until Bailey Mill.

Longtown and 500 metres later cross a bridge over the Sark into England. Views of the Cumbrian fells appear here. Continue for 2 miles through Silverhill Woods and past Oakbank Lakes to reach the **A7**, which must unfortunately be followed with care rightwards for a mile into **Longtown**, crossing a bridge over the **Esk** – a river that marked the edge of the Debateable Lands. ◄

At the far southern end of Longtown, by the war memorial, look out for a right turn on the 7 signed to The Fauld. Take this, passing **Arthuret Church**, where Archie Armstrong, favoured court jester of James I and Charles I, is buried. Opposite the church is a layby and plaque commemorating the site of the Battle of Solway Moss.

> The 1542 **Battle of Solway Moss** is renowned for being the undoing of James V of Scotland. The Grahams – Reivers from the English West March – were instrumental in inflicting defeat. James himself was not present at the battle, but rather ensconced in nearby Lochmaben Castle, allegedly at the behest of his heavily pregnant wife. James' humiliation at the battle worsened his already faltering state

The Borderers Ride – Gretna to Berwick-upon-Tweed

of health. He lasted only two weeks longer – just long enough to meet his baby daughter who later became Mary Queen of Scots.

After another mile, look out for an easy-to-miss signed 7 cycle path which leaves the road to the right straight after the entrance to a scrapyard. Take this former railway path, crossing a bridge over the **River Lyne** and emerging 300 metres later at a road heading into **Westlinton**. It is here that the Borderers Ride joins the Reivers Route by turning left.

The rest of the day follows the description and mapping for Day 2 of the Reivers Route to finish in **Bailey Mill**.

Day 2: Bailey Mill to Bellingham
Start: Bailey Mill (NY 517 785), **Finish:** Bellingham (TQ 374 717), **Distance:** 37 miles (60km), **Ascent:** 875m
This stage is exactly the same as Day 3 of the Reivers Route: see that stage for route description and mapping.

Day 3: Bellingham to Wooler
Start: Bellingham (TQ 374 717), **Finish:** Wooler (NT 991 281), **Distance:** 45 miles (72km), **Ascent:** 1092m
In **Bellingham**, turn right at the post office on the main street and follow signs for the 10 and 68. Continue straight on towards West Woodburn (the Reivers Route takes a right turn less than 100 metres after the bridge).

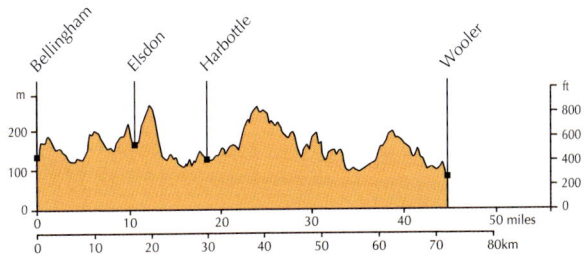

Cycling the Reivers Route

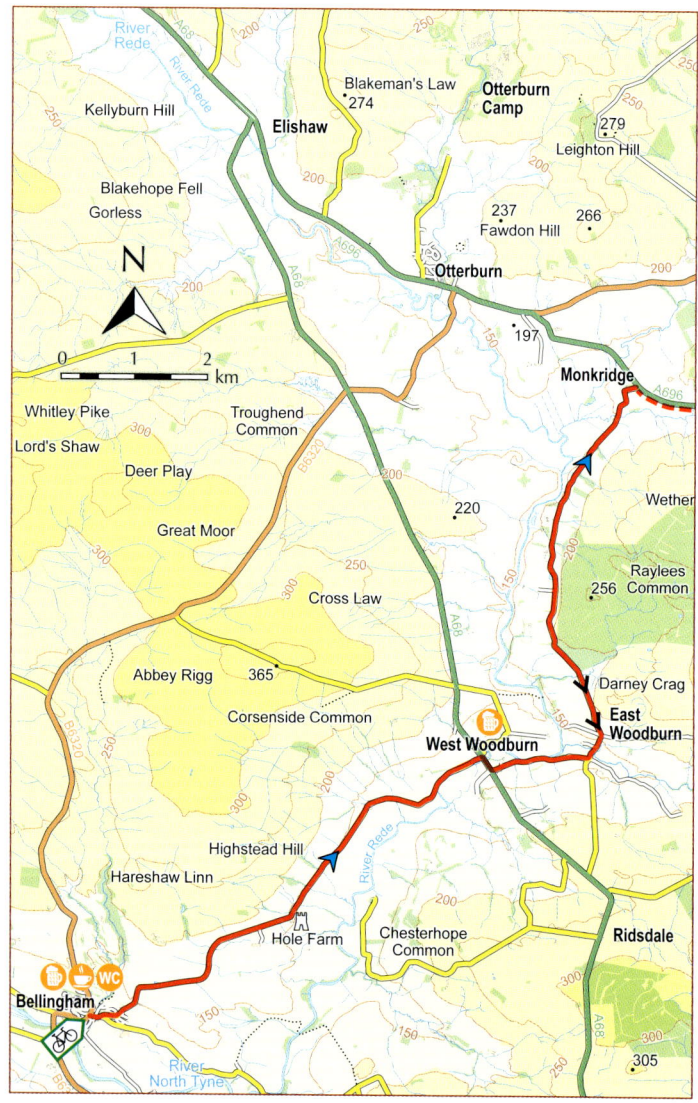

THE BORDERERS RIDE – GRETNA TO BERWICK-UPON-TWEED

The 68 heads uphill out of town, momentarily sharing its course with the Pennine Way.

The route continues through Redesdale, running roughly parallel to the **River Rede**, past small former mine workings and a tiny tarn. A prominent bastle, in a raised position, can be seen on the right behind **Hole Farm** on the first descent, while another bastle is incorporated into the next farm on the left. The route rejoins the riverside just outside West Woodburn, where the remains – merely earthworks – of the Roman fort of Habitancum, notably north of Hadrian's Wall, are on the hillside to the right.

At **West Woodburn**, turn right on a traffic-calmed section of the A68 for less than 100 metres before a left turn to **East Woodburn** is taken. Continue on the same road round through the village which is followed by a fairly stiff climb up the side of **Darney Crag** and a great flatter section skirting Blaxter Bog Forest.

Descend gently past a small tarn on a gated section with expansive moorland views beside the River Rede once more. The road meets the A696 at **Monkridge**. **Do not cross**, but instead turn right onto a shared-use contraflow pavement cycle path which is followed for nearly a mile until it ends at a sign for Elsdon. Cross the A-road carefully and take the splendid minor road that climbs over the western fringe of Castle Hill before dropping into the delightful village of **Elsdon** and the Northumberland National Park.

Map continues on page 100

Entering Elsdon and the Northumberland National Park

ELSDON

Elsdon, once the capital of Redesdale, seems to ooze history from every wall and building. The 11th-century Elsdon Castle is also known as the Mote Hills. It was built by Robert de Umfraville during William the Conqueror's reign. William gave Robert the Lordship of Redesdale and excused him from military service in return for keeping the frontier in this vicinity free from raiders and wolves. A number of dead from the nearby Anglo-Scottish Battle of Otterburn, 1388, appear to have been buried in a communal grave in the churchyard. Elsdon's easily spotted medieval pele tower dates back to the year of Agincourt, 1415, when Henry V was on the throne. It is now a private home.

Cycling the Reivers Route

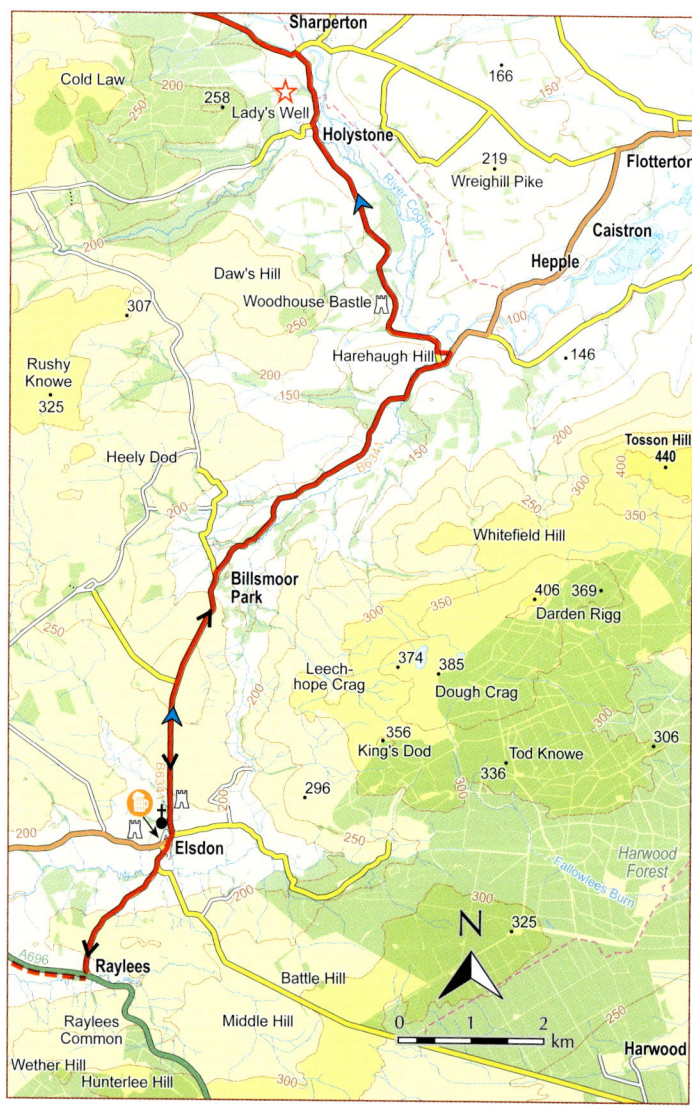

The Borderers Ride – Gretna to Berwick-upon-Tweed

Looking across Coquetdale to the Simonside hills and Harwood Forest

Continue past the village greens, and at the junction by the church turn right (a left leads to the Bird in Bush pub). Around 200 metres after the turning there is a spot to pull in and look at the impressive and imposing earthworks and ruins of the motte-and-bailey **Elsdon Castle**, which loom above the road. Up the short lane on the left before the castle, Elsdon's impressive inhabited pele tower can also be seen.

The climb out of Elsdon is the hardest on-road ascent of the day. The reward for cresting the top is an expansive view of the northern Pennines and Cheviots. From this elevated position, four pleasant miles of cycling lead down past Harwood Forest and **Billsmoor Park**, to where a well-marked left turn at **Harehaugh**, signed to Holystone and Harbottle, is taken. A mile after the turning is **Woodhouse Bastle**. The bastle can be seen 100 metres to the left of the road. The route has now joined Coquetdale and the **River Coquet** can be seen to the right for the next few miles. ▶

Continue to the hamlet of **Holystone**, where a micro-detour to the tiny National Trust-owned **Lady's Well** makes a good sandwich stop.

Woodhouse Bastle is visible from the route and worth an up-close visit with a two-minute walk.

Map continues on page 103

Lady's Well is a small lake with a cross and a statue, which is a few minutes off route via a signed walk. The Holy Well was a watering place on the Roman road between the east coast and Redesdale. It was named Lady's Well when a priory of Augustinian canonesses was built in Holystone during the early 12th century.

A mile after Holystone, turn left at a T-junction and follow the road for a further 1½ miles to the village of **Harbottle** (pub), which also makes a pleasant stop.

HARBOTTLE CASTLE

Harbottle Castle is free to explore, and can be accessed from the designated castle car park 100 metres west of the village houses, where a child's poem has been carved in stone. The castle was built by the Umfraville family in the 12th century to strengthen Henry II's border defences. It changed hands between English and Scots forces in this period, then became the base of Warden Thomas Dacre during the height of the Reivers' activities in the early 16th century. Dacre only added fuel to the fire of disputes in the region, which carried on past the Union of the Crowns. Another notable resident was Margaret Tudor, sister of Henry VIII and widow of James IV of Scotland, who was granted asylum to stay here.

After another mile, cross **Alwinton** Bridge over the River Coquet and continue to a second bridge (Alwinton, a worthwhile stop, can be seen just off route).

Sir Walter Scott stayed at the **Rose and Thistle Inn** in Alwinton while he penned the classic historical novel and trans-border tale *Rob Roy* (1817). The inn is open daily, just off route. Indeed, an unlikely pub crawl in this remote setting is possible as **Clennell Hall hotel** is also open daily. The Hall has developed over the centuries from a 16th-century pele tower. The original cellar of the tower is still in use.

There are now two onward options. For the primary (on-road) route: before the second bridge is crossed, take

THE BORDERERS RIDE – GRETNA TO BERWICK-UPON-TWEED

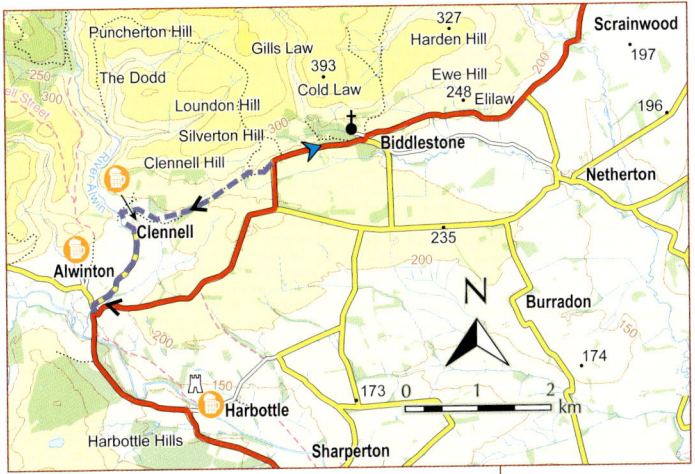

a sharp right turn with a switchback at a triangular junction and climb gradually for over a mile, eventually taking a left signed to **Biddlestone**.

Map continues on page 104

Off-road alternative

For the alternative (off-road) route: cross the second bridge and, 25 metres later, turn right on a dead-end road signed to Clennell. Take a right at a split through the caravan site, at the rear of which a more pronounced track can be joined. Bear rightwards through a wood and continue for 2 miles to rejoin the on-road route with a left (effectively straight on) before **Biddlestones** Farm.

> **Biddlestone** gains its name from a Neolithic stone circle, remnants of which can still be seen near Biddlestone Chapel. The chapel, hidden on the left in the trees just after the farm turning, incorporated a 14th-century pele tower during its construction in 1820.

From Biddlestone, turn left at a junction signed to Biddlestone Town Foot, then almost immediately swing

Cycling the Reivers Route

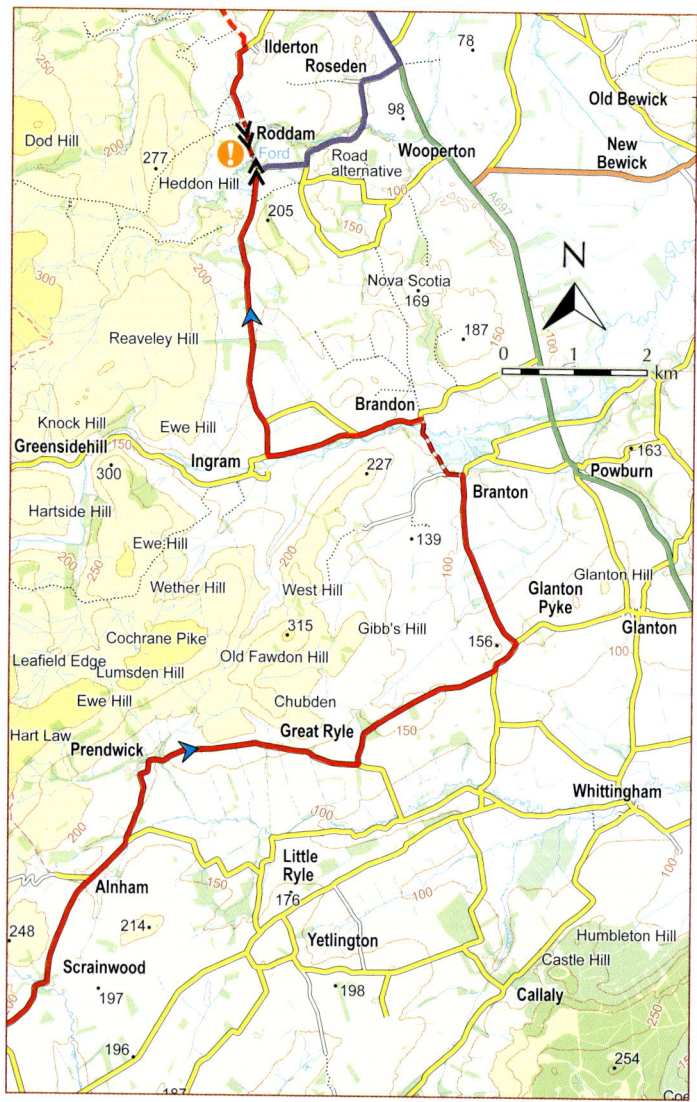

Crossing the River Breamish between the hamlets of Branton and Brandon

right onto a fantastic tiny single-track road. This has gates and a tricky dip which can be muddy. Continue straight, passing through the hamlet of **Elilaw** and bearing left at Scrainwood Farm, before eventually passing the hamlet of **Alnham**. Continue straight ahead through **Prendwick** and staying on the dominant road towards Powburn (which is not actually reached).

After nearly 4 miles of gentle rolling farm and moorland, a left turn is made onto a narrower road at a fingerpost signing Branton, Fawdon and Ingram. At **Branton** there begins a section of the 68 that has been contrived using off-road bridleways and byways to prevent cyclists having to use the busy A697 on their way to Wooler. At the T-junction in Branton, turn left then branch right after 100 metres, passing a reservoir to reach a footbridge over the **River Breamish** which connects Branton with its twin hamlet of **Brandon**. Turn left where the track from the footbridge emerges at a road and continue for a couple of lovely miles by the river towards Ingram. ▶

The remote hamlet of Ingram surprisingly has a national park visitor centre (toilet, café). It is reached with a left over the bridge and left again.

Take a right turn before Ingram with 68 cycle signs. This road, which gives views of the Cheviot (815m) to the west, is followed for nearly 3 miles, past a small

Map continues on page 107

Cycling the Reivers Route

A short bike push is the crux of the off-road section by Roddam

tarn to the crux 500-metre off-road section of the day near **Roddam**. (This can be avoided – see the following description – although the road alternative involves a two-mile stretch on the relatively busy A697.)

Take a left to leave the road at a corner with 68 signage and a warning for a ford. Most tourers will dismount for the steep and usually muddy descent to cross Roddam Burn. Take the path onto the footbridge to avoid the ford and its steep exit on the other side. Rest assured the difficulties do not last long. After a short, grassy rideable section, the route rejoins a surfaced road at Ilderton Moor Farm – phew!

After a mile on this road reach the hamlet of **Ilderton** and turn left at the crossroads onto a byway. This becomes a track – rideable, although care is needed with the loose surface. Avoid the ford over Lilburn Burn by using the footbridge on the left. Having ridden this off-road section, turn right where it meets another minor road on a bend

The Borderers Ride – Gretna to Berwick-upon-Tweed

and in 200 metres turn left, signed as the 68 to reach **North Middleton** in 400 metres.

Road alternative

Ignore the 68 and ford signage, instead continuing through the hamlet of Roddam. Turn left at the T-junction. After a pleasant mile, keep right at a T-junction (left is a dead end) to meet the **A697**. Turn left on this and continue for 2 miles before taking the second exit left; this is signed to North and South Middleton. Keep straight on to be met by the off-road route at North Middleton.

Continue through North Middleton and across a shallow ford on the road over Coldgate Water in an area known

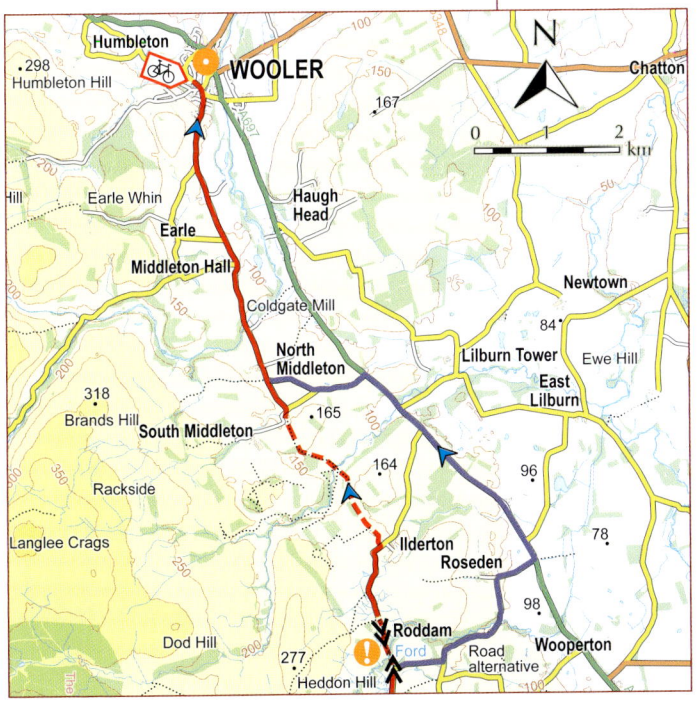

Cycling the Reivers Route

WOOLER

Wooler, like so many of the settlements in this vicinity, was for centuries subject to the toing and froing of border conflicts; lost medieval forts and castles litter the surrounding hillsides, especially to the west. In 1402 the Battle of Holmedon Hill took place just over a mile to the north-west of Wooler. A convincing victory for the English over the Scots, the battle is celebrated in Shakespeare's *Henry IV, Part I*: 'Ten thousand bold Scots, two-and-twenty knights / Balk'd in their own blood, did Sir Walter see / On Holmedon's plains.' Wooler is a great little town to stop in for the night, with a range of decent accommodation and eating options.

Crossing Weetwood Bridge after leaving Wooler

as Happy Valley. From here it is straightforward cycling, albeit with a last haul uphill before a steep descent is made to meet the high street in **Wooler**.

Day 4: Wooler to Berwick-upon-Tweed
Start: Wooler (NT 991 281), **Finish:** Berwick-upon-Tweed (NU 009 524) **Distance:** 34 miles (55km), **Ascent:** 483m
From the south-eastern end of the High Street in **Wooler**, head down Church Street to carefully cross the **A697** and pass over a narrow bridge opposite. Continue out of town, following 68 signage. The short stretch on this B-road is one of the busier sections of the whole route, but is mercifully over quickly. In 1¼ miles take an obvious left turn onto a minor road with a narrow stone bridge over the **River Till**. Head uphill.

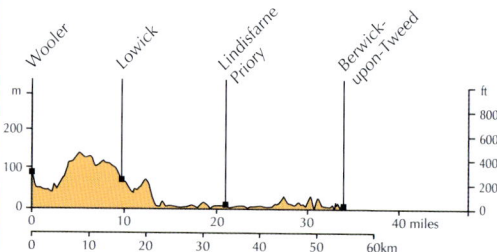

Map continues on page 112

THE BORDERERS RIDE – GRETNA TO BERWICK-UPON-TWEED

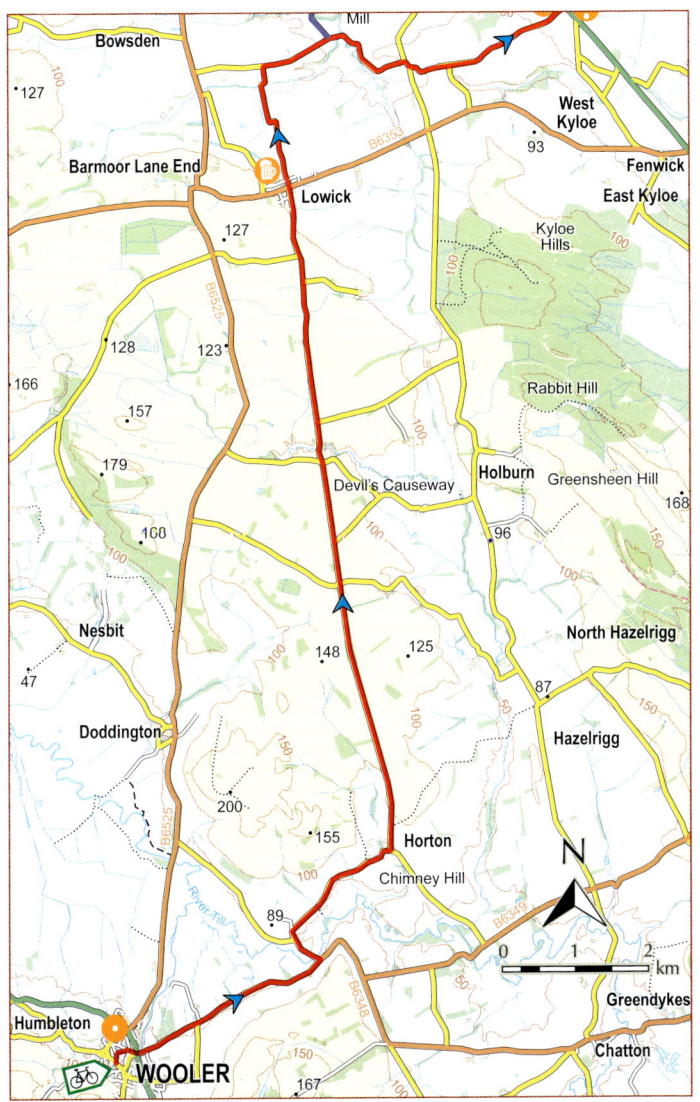

The Devil's Causeway between Horton and Lowick

The Borderers Ride now **parts company with the 68**, which splits off left after a few hundred metres. Stay straight on for another 1½ miles to **Horton**. At the eastern end of the village, take a left signed to Lowick and Ancroft. This is an old Roman road called the **Devil's Causeway**. It gives sea and hill views and is a fantastically quiet and simple way to reach **Lowick** in 5½ miles and eventually connect with the coastal NCN 1 route.

The **Devil's Causeway** is thought to predate Hadrian's Wall. It was unusual in that it was only used for cavalry rather than marching men. Its name comes from the Saxons, who were superstitious about the strange stone-built ramp crossing their territories. It was used by both advancing English and Scottish armies over centuries including by the English, nominally under the regency control of Catherine of Aragon, while heading north to face James IV of Scotland at the Battle of Flodden in 1513.

Having reached the crossroads at Lowick (pub, shop), go straight across the B6353 and continue another mile in the same direction with views east to Lindisfarne. Turn right at the next T-junction, then after another 1km bear right at a triangular junction to pass through **Lowick Mill**. ▶

At the next junction turn right, signed to Lowick and Holborn, then almost immediately turn left towards Beal. The next crossroads is with the **A1** – here not even a dual carriageway. There is a pub at this junction. Cross with care and continue on a contraflow cycle path to **Beal**, passing over a level crossing and with a little climb into the small village which has a licensed café-style restaurant.

At the edge of Beal, the off-road route north to Berwick leaves the road. Continue straight on to visit Holy Island. The decision to visit may be entirely dependent upon tide times, which are posted at the beginning

For road bikers not visiting Holy Island, the onward route splits off left at the triangular junction – see the following 'Road alternative' description.

Sea views on the route beyond Lowick

Lindisfarne Castle perched on its volcanic mound

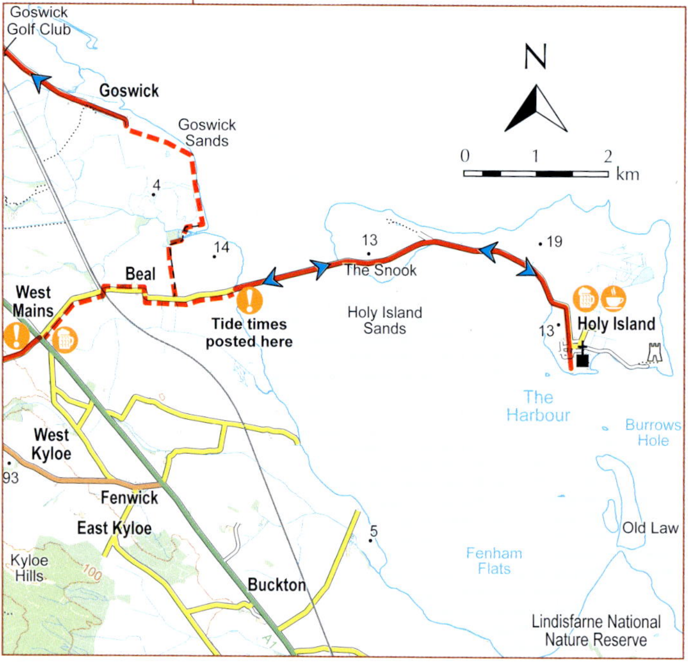

112

of the causeway 700 metres further along the road. Bear in mind that crossing the causeway and riding to the village and castle on Holy Island is an 8-mile round trip (included in the overall route distance). Although it is flat, the stretch across the tidal plain can be windy and surprisingly busy with tourist traffic.

> **You must consult the tide timetable before crossing the Lindisfarne causeway**. This is posted beside the road but can be viewed in advance at holyislandcrossingtimes.northumberland.gov.uk.

Map continues on page 114

LINDISFARNE

The Holy Island of Lindisfarne is renowned as a place of religious significance. Irish monk St Aidan founded a priory here in 634, after being granted the island by Northumbrian King Oswald. The priory was presided over by St Cuthbert before his death on the nearby Farne Island in 685. Thereafter, the island became a centre of Christianity for the north of England before being raided by the Vikings in 793 – an event nominally viewed as the dawn of the Viking Age in northern England. The monks only actually evacuated in the face of sustained Viking invasion in 875. The priory was then re-established in 1093 and was later fortified to protect it from Border skirmishes during the 13th and 14th centuries. Ruins dating from the 12th century can be visited today, along with a museum. Lindisfarne Castle was built in the 16th century using some stone from the priory, which had been suppressed under Henry VIII during the dissolution of the monasteries.

The main NCN Route 1 continues to Berwick, splitting off northwards from the cycle path near the roadside 700 metres before the start of the Lindisfarne causeway. This is a wonderfully atmospheric yet time-consuming last few miles into Berwick which can be very muddy and slow going. ▶

The gravel path soon disappears as a small bridge is crossed and the route continues along the grassy seashore plains on a narrow and sometimes surprisingly indistinct path. Watch out for roaming cattle on the gated

Road bikers should retrace the route to Lowick Mill and then head straight on (right) at the triangular junction for a mile before turning left towards Ancroft.

CYCLING THE REIVERS ROUTE

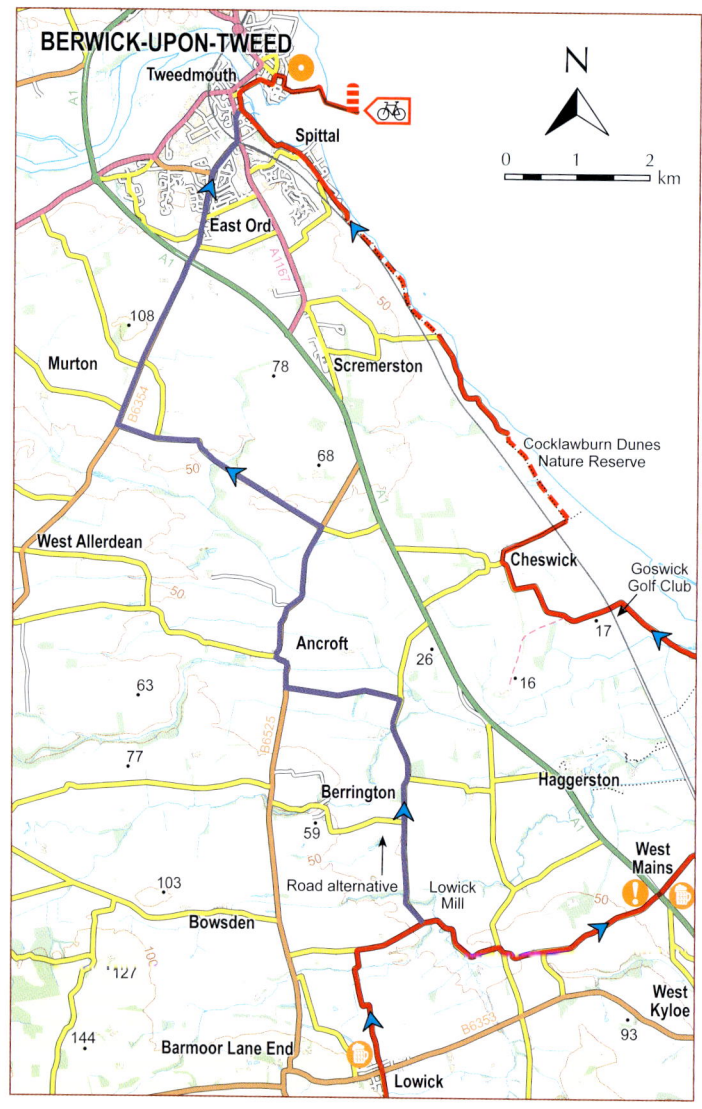

The Borderers Ride – Gretna to Berwick-upon-Tweed

route which eventually emerges onto a surfaced road at Beachcomber House, where there is a campsite.

Continue on past **Goswick** golf course, after which the route turns briefly inland, crossing a railway. A mile later, take a signed right turn swinging back towards the coast. The road deteriorates on crossing over the railway to arrive at a small dead-end parking area with access to a lovely beach. From here, the cycle route heads leftwards, at first on a good dune-side path which later becomes grassy and prone to mud with roaming cattle once again.

Pass a small tarn and continue the wild coastal riding until tarmac returns at the parking area for **Cocklawburn Dunes Nature Reserve** where there is a World War 2 gun emplacement looking out over the North Sea. The coast takes on a more rugged craggy nature, with the rock formations at Middle and Near Skerrs visible. Spectacular cliff and sea views continue all the way to Berwick.

After a mile on the clifftop road, take the signed track right at a bend for a memorable stretch of off-road riding above the impressive and vertiginous coastline on a grassy, often rutted and narrow path. The route never strays too close to the precipitous drops, but take care here for the next 1½ miles, after which a tarmac road is met. Continue straight on this, dropping down almost to sea level.

Where the urban area of Berwick begins at a small car park with a stone welcoming you to the town, the signed Route 1 goes straight ahead. However, a much better option is to immediately cut down a short ramp to connect to the promenade and ride along that towards town and Spittal Beach.

At the end of the paved promenade, continue on the seafront for a further 200 metres past an old chimney and across another car park. Follow Sandstell Road to a crossroads where a right turn rejoins Route 1.

Road alternative

Bear left at the triangular junction (or right if you've retraced the route from Lindisfarne) and take the second left signed to Ancroft (after 2 miles). Turn right onto the

B6525 through **Ancroft**, then over a mile later turn left at an unsigned crossroads. Stay straight on to intersect the **B6354**. Turn right and then continue to reach Berwick in a further 3 miles. Take care where this road crosses the **A1** and join the off-road route at the Tweedmouth rail bridge.

In **Tweedmouth**, where the road goes beneath a rail bridge, continue straight ahead on a narrow lane to reach a T-junction. Dogleg left, right, then left again to reach the Tweed, before some small docks.

Cycle past the small docks with great views of Berwick's famous town walls, along with its lighthouse and bridges. Merge right at a junction onto Main Street.

A fitting end to the ride at the sea proper is to continue to finish at Berwick's lighthouse on the pier. Unfortunately, the shapely early 17th-century 15-span Berwick Bridge is one way, so dismount to use the pedestrian pavement over the bridge. Turn right to access the promenade on the medieval Berwick Walls fortification.

After 450 metres, just beyond a cannon on the ramparts (captured from the Russians at the Battle of Sebastopol in 1854), take a ramp to the left down to meet Ness Street. Turn right under the ramparts onto Pier Road and, passing an easily accessed tiny shale beach, use the windswept pier to reach the **lighthouse** – a spectacular conclusion to a tour well done.

The end of the route: Berwick lighthouse at low tide

BERWICK-UPON-TWEED

Berwick's old and new road bridges and George Stephenson's rail bridge of 1852 beyond

The Archbishop of Glasgow's 'Curse of the Reivers' of 1525 promises the Reivers that 'the water of the Tweed and other rivers that they ride shall drown them'. Lying at the mouth of the Tweed, Berwick is an especially fitting place to end the Borderers Ride. The town was fought over by the English and Scots throughout the medieval and Tudor periods, during which time it changed hands 12 times. The impressive town walls were built by 'Hammer of the Scots' Edward I after he captured Berwick in 1296. Edward even displayed a dismembered arm of 'Braveheart' William Wallace in Berwick at this time. Nonetheless, its fortifications did not stop the town from returning to Scottish rule almost as soon as they were finished in 1318. An apocryphal yet popular story about Berwick remaining at war with Russia after the settlement of the Crimean conflict adds to the historically dramatic mystique of the town. The story goes that Queen Victoria declared war in her official capacity of monarch of 'Great Britain, Ireland, Berwick-upon-Tweed and the British Dominions beyond the Sea'. When peace was declared, the name of Berwick was omitted from the paperwork and the oversight was not discovered until 1914, leading to a separate treaty hastily being signed. Berwick's 'otherness' was enshrined in Royal Proclamations during the 16th and 17th centuries, where it was mentioned as being 'of the kingdom, but not in it'. While today Berwick has an unquestionably English character, its football team nonetheless plays in the Scottish League.

APPENDIX A
Accommodation

Location	Type	Name	Phone	Website	Evening meal available	En route	Bike storage
Whitehaven	Hotel	Chase	01946 693656	chasewhitehaven.co.uk	Yes	Yes	Yes
Whitehaven	Guest house	Glenard	01946 692249			Yes	
Workington	Hotel	Morven House	01900 602118		Yes	Yes	Yes
Workington	B&B	Dower House	01900 605906	dowerhouse-workington.co.uk		Close by	Yes
Caldbeck	Pub	Oddfellows Arms	01697 478227	oddfellows-caldbeck.co.uk	Yes	Yes	Yes
Caldbeck	B&B	Old Rectory	01697 478484	www.oldrectorycaldbeck.co.uk	At pub	Yes	Yes
Caldbeck	Camping	Caldbeck camping	016974 78367	www.caldbeckcamping.co.uk	At pub	Yes	
Hesket Newmarket	B&B	Denton House	01697 478415	www.dentonhouseguesthouse.co.uk	At pub	Yes	Yes
Hesket Newmarket	Camping	Greenhill Farm	01697 478453		At pub	Yes	
Dalston	Camping	Cardewlees	07539 144194	www.campingatcardewlees.com		< 2km	

Appendix A – Accommodation

Location	Type	Name	Phone	Website	Evening meal available	En route	Bike storage
Dalston	Cabins	Thornfield	01228 319028	www.thornfieldcamping cabins.co.uk	At pub	Yes	
Carlisle	Camping	Roman Wall	07784 736423	hadrians-wall-accommodation.co.uk	At pub	5km on 72	
Carlisle	Camping	Dandy Dinmont	01228 674611			5km	
Carlisle	Hotel	Crown and Mitre	01228 525491	www.crownandmitre-hotel-carlisle.com	Yes	Yes	
Carlisle	Guest house	Hazel Dean	01228 711953		Yes	Yes	Yes
Carlisle	B&B	Tantallon	01228 550209			2km	
Carlisle	Hostel	City Hostel	07914 720821	carlislecityhostel.com		Nearby	Yes
Westlinton	B&B	Glen	07766 027162		Yes	Yes	
Westlinton	B&B	Lynebank	01228 792820		Yes	Yes	Yes
Longtown	Hotel	Sycamore Tree	01228 791919	thesycamoretreelongtown.co.uk	Yes	4km	
Bailey Mill	Self-catering, B&B and camping	Bailey Mill	01697 748617	bailey-mill.co.uk	Yes	Yes	Yes
Sorbietrees	B&B	Sorbietrees	01387 375215	www.sorbietrees.co.uk	Lift to pub	2km/Yes	Yes
Kershopefoot	B&B/self-catering	Abbotshaw	01387 375 928	www.abbotshawhouse.co.uk		2km	Yes

CYCLING THE REIVERS ROUTE

Location	Type	Name	Phone	Website	Evening meal available	En route	Bike storage
Newcastleton	Hotel	Grapes	01387 375245	thegrapeshotel.co.uk	Yes	5km/Yes	Yes
Newcastleton	Hotel	Liddesdale	01387 375255	theliddesdalehotel.co.uk	Yes	5km/Yes	Yes
Kielder	Camping	Kielder	01434 239257	kieldercampsite.co.uk	At pub poss, shop	5km/Yes	
Stannersburn	Pub B&B	Pheasant Inn	01434 240382	www.thepheasantinn.com	Yes	2km	
Charlton	Camping	Bow Rigg	01434 240663	theboerigg.co.uk	Yes on site	2km	
Thorneyburn	Glamping huts	Wild Northumbrian	01669 650166	www.wildnorthumbrian.co.uk		Yes	
Lanehead	Group self-catering	Tarset Tor	01434 240980	www.tarset-tor.co.uk		Yes	
Bellingham	Camping, self-catering	Demesne Farm	01434 220258	demesnefarmcampsite.co.uk	At pub	Yes	
Bellingham	Camping	Bellingham	01434 220175	www.campingandcaravanningclub.co.uk	At pub	Yes	
Bellingham	Hotel	Riverdale Hall	01434 220254	www.riverdalehallhotel.co.uk	Yes	Yes	Yes
Bellingham	B&B	Fountain Cottage	07753 162465	fountain-cottage.com	Yes	Yes	
Bellingham	B&B	Lyndale	01434 220361		At pub	Yes	

Appendix A – Accommodation

Location	Type	Name	Phone	Website	Evening meal available	En route	Bike storage
Bellingham	B&B	The Barn	01434 220744	www.thebarnandbbellingham.co.uk	At pub	Yes	Yes
Bellingham	B&B	Bridgeford Farm	01434 220940	www.bridgefordfarmbandb.co.uk		3km	Yes
West Woodburn	Pub B&B	Bay Horse	01434 270218	bayhorseinn.org	Yes	Yes	
Raylees	B&B, camping	Ravenscleugh	01830 520896	www.ravenscleugh.com		Yes	
Otterburn	B&B	Butterchurn	01830 520 585	www.butterchurnguesthouse.com	At pub	5km	
Stamfordham	Pub B&B	Plough	01661 853555	www.theploughstamfordham.co.uk	Yes	2km	
Ponteland	Hotel and pub	Diamond Inn	01661 872898	thediamondinn.co.uk	Yes	Yes	
Tynemouth	B&B	No 61	0191 2573687	no61.co.uk	Nearby	Yes	
Tynemouth	Hotel	Park	0191 2571406	parkhoteltynemouth.co.uk	Yes	Yes	
Additional accommodation for the Borderers Ride							
Gretna	B&B	Surrone House	01461 338341	www.surronehouse.co.uk		Yes	
Gretna	B&B	Prince Charlie's	01461 337272	princecharlies.co.uk		Yes	
Alwinton	Pub	Rose and Thistle	01669 650226	roseandthistlealwinton.com	Yes	Yes	

CYCLING THE REIVERS ROUTE

Location	Type	Name	Phone	Website	Evening meal available	En route	Bike storage
Clennell	Hotel	Clennell Hall	01669 650377	www.clennellhallcountryhouse.com	Yes	1km	
Branton	B&B	Bosk	01665 660129	www.breamishvalley.co.uk		Yes	
Ingram	B&B	Ingram House	01665 578906	ingram-house.com		Yes	
Wooler	YHA	Wooler YHA	0345 2602931	www.yha.org.uk	At pub	Yes	Yes
Wooler	Pub B&B	Black Bull	01668 281309		Yes	Yes	
Wooler	Hotel	Tankerville Arms	01668 281581	tankervillehotel.co.uk	Yes	Yes	
Wooler	B&B	Noble Lands	07740 883378		At pub	Yes	
Wooler	B&B	Old Mill	01668 283349	www.theoldmillwooler.co.uk	At pub	Yes	
Wooler	Camping	Highburn House	01668 281344	highburn-house.co.uk		Yes	
Lowick	Pub B&B	White Swan	01289 388249	thewhiteswanlowick.co.uk	Yes	Yes	
Lowick	Pub B&B	Black Bull	01289 388375	blackbulllowick.co.uk	Yes	Yes	
Berwick-upon-Tweed	YHA	Berwick YHA	0345 371 9676	www.yha.org.uk	Yes	Yes	Yes
Berwick-upon-Tweed	Camping	Seaview	01289 305198	www.caravanclub.co.uk		Yes	
Berwick-upon-Tweed	B&B	Castle Vale	01289 303699	castlevalebandb.co.uk	At pub	Yes	
Berwick-upon-Tweed	Pub B&B	King's Head	01289 331491	www.kingsheadberwick.co.uk	Yes	Yes	

APPENDIX B
Bike shops and other useful contacts

Bike shops in route order

Whitehaven
Haven Cycles
2 Preston Street
LA1 1NZ
tel 01946 63236
havencycles-c2cservices.co.uk

Workington
Halfords
Derwent Dr Retail Park
CA14 3YW
tel 01900 601635
www.halfords.com

Cockermouth
Cyclewise
Unit 2
Fairfield Buildings
CA13 9RU
tel 01900 821998
cyclewise.co.uk

4Play Cycles
25–31 Market Place
CA13 9NH
tel 01900 823377
www.4playcycles.co.uk

Qwink
9 Vicarage Ln
Cockermouth
CA13 9DG
tel 07447 642513
qwink.co.uk

Carlisle
Scotby Cycles
Church St
CA2 5TL
tel 01228 546931
www.scotbycycles.co.uk

Palace Cycles
120–124 Botchergate
CA1 1SH
tel 01228 523142
palacecycles.co.uk

Bikeseven
1 Market Street
tel 01228 739926
www.bikeseven.co.uk

Longtown
Bikeseven
Unit 2 Sandilands
CA6 5LY
tel 01228 792497
www.bikeseven.co.uk

Leaplish
The Bike Place
Kielder Waterside
NE48 1BT
tel 01434 250144
www.thebikeplace.co.uk

Kielder village
The Bike Place
Kielder Cycle Centre
NE48 1ER
tel 01434 250457
www.thebikeplace.co.uk

North Shields
Tyne Cycles
19–20 Rudyerd St
NE29 6RR
tel 0191 2592266
www.tynecycles.co.uk

Tynemouth
Whiptail Cycles
3 Livingstone View
NE30 2PL
tel 0191 2572212
www.whiptail-cycles.co.uk

Additional bike shops on the Borderers Ride

Wooler
Haugh Head Garage
NE71 6QP
tel 01668 281316
haughheadgarage.co.uk

Berwick-upon-Tweed
Berwick Cycles
17A Bridge St
TD15 1ES
tel 01289 331476
berwickcycles.co.uk

Planetary14 Bikes mobile repairs
tel 07546 937700
planetary14bikes.co.uk

Cycle/baggage transport
Pedal Power
tel 01665 713448 or 07790 596782
pedal-power.co.uk

The Bicycle Transport Co
tel 01297 240400
www.thebicycletransportcompany.co.uk

Eco Cycle Adventures
tel 01434 610076
www.ecocycleadventures.co.uk

The Bike Bus Stanley Travel
tel 01207 237424
stanley-travel.com/the-bike-bus

Companies that arrange accommodation and transport as a package
Trailbrakes
tel 01416 286676 or 07922 653327
www.trailbrakes.co.uk

CycleActive
tel 01768 840400
cycleactive.com

APPENDIX C
Further reading

Crofton, Ian, *Walking the Border* (Birlinn, 2014)

Moffat, Alistair, *The Reivers* (Birlinn, 2011)

Robb, Graham, *The Debatable Land: The Lost World Between Scotland and England* (Picador, 2018)

Scott, Sir Walter, ed., *Minstrelsy of the Scottish Border* (1802, with later editions to 1830) is an anthology of collected border ballads by one of the 19th century's most successful authors. Various reprint-style editions are available. One by BiblioBazaar, 2006, is reasonable. However, original editions of the anthology can be viewed online or downloaded for free at archive.org, see: archive.org/details/minstrelsyscotti01scotiala

Stewart, Rory, *The Marches: Border walks with my father* (London: Penguin, 2016)

The English Heritage report on the Battle of Solway Moss makes for fascinating reading. It is available here in PDF form: historicengland.org.uk/content/docs/listing/battlefields/solway-moss

Thompson, Patricia, 'The Murder of Thomas Davidson': morbidology.com/the-murder-of-thomas-davidson

Turnbull, Ronald, *Walking in the Scottish Borders* (Cicerone, 2020)

Crossing the border at Scotch Knowe deep in Kershope Forest

DOWNLOAD THE ROUTES IN GPX FORMAT

All the routes in this guide are available for download from:

www.cicerone.co.uk/910/GPX

as GPX files. You should be able to load them into most formats of mobile device, whether GPS or smartphone.

When you go to this link, you will be asked for your email address and where you purchased the guide, and have the option to subscribe to the Cicerone e-newsletter.

www.cicerone.co.uk

CICERONE'S NORTHERN UK GUIDES

BRITISH ISLES CHALLENGES, COLLECTIONS AND ACTIVITIES

Cycling Land's End to John o' Groats
The Big Rounds
The Book of the Bothy
The C2C Cycle Route
The End to End Cycle Route
The Mountains of England and Wales: Vol 1 Wales
The Mountains of England and Wales: Vol 2 England
The National Trails
Walking The End to End Trail

SCOTLAND

Backpacker's Britain: Northern Scotland
Ben Nevis and Glen Coe
Cycle Touring in Northern Scotland
Cycling in the Hebrides
Great Mountain Days in Scotland
Mountain Biking in Southern and Central Scotland
Mountain Biking in West and North West Scotland
Not the West Highland Way
Scotland
Scotland's Best Small Mountains
Scotland's Mountain Ridges
Skye's Cuillin Ridge Traverse
The Ayrshire and Arran Coastal Paths
The Borders Abbeys Way
The Great Glen Way
The Great Glen Way Map Booklet
The Hebridean Way
The Hebrides
The Isle of Mull
The Isle of Skye
The Skye Trail
The Southern Upland Way
The Speyside Way
The Speyside Way Map Booklet
The West Highland Way
The West Highland Way Map Booklet
Walking Highland Perthshire
Walking in the Cairngorms
Walking in the Pentland Hills
Walking in the Scottish Borders
Walking in the Southern Uplands
Walking in Torridon
Walking Loch Lomond and the Trossachs
Walking on Arran
Walking on Harris and Lewis
Walking on Jura, Islay and Colonsay
Walking on Rum and the Small Isles
Walking on the Orkney and Shetland Isles
Walking on Uist and Barra
Walking the Cape Wrath Trail
Walking the Corbetts
  Vol 1 South of the Great Glen
  Vol 2 North of the Great Glen
Walking the Galloway Hills
Walking the Munros
  Vol 1 – Southern, Central and Western Highlands
  Vol 2 – Northern Highlands and the Cairngorms
Winter Climbs Ben Nevis and Glen Coe
Winter Climbs in the Cairngorms

NORTHERN ENGLAND TRAILS

Hadrian's Wall Path
Hadrian's Wall Path Map Booklet
The Coast to Coast Walk
The Coast to Coast Walk Map Booklet
The Dales Way
The Dales Way Map Booklet
The Pennine Way
The Pennine Way Map Booklet
Walking the Tour of the Lake District

NORTH EAST ENGLAND, YORKSHIRE DALES AND PENNINES

Cycling in the Yorkshire Dales
Great Mountain Days in the Pennines
Mountain Biking in the Yorkshire Dales
St Oswald's Way and St Cuthbert's Way
The Cleveland Way and the Yorkshire Wolds Way
The Cleveland Way Map Booklet
The North York Moors
The Reivers Way
The Teesdale Way
Trail and Fell Running in the Yorkshire Dales
Walking in County Durham
Walking in Northumberland
Walking in the North Pennines
Walking in the Yorkshire Dales: North and East
Walking in the Yorkshire Dales: South and West

NORTH WEST ENGLAND THE ISLE OF MAN

Cycling the Pennine Bridleway
Cycling the Way of the Roses
Hadrian's Cycleway
Isle of Man Coastal Path
The Lancashire Cycleway
The Lune Valley and Howgills
Walking in Cumbria's Eden Valley
Walking in Lancashire
Walking in the Forest of Bowland and Pendle
Walking on the Isle of Man
Walking on the West Pennine Moors
Walks in Silverdale and Arnside

LAKE DISTRICT

Cycling in the Lake District
Great Mountain Days in the Lake District
Lake District Winter Climbs
Lake District: High Level and Fell Walks
Lake District: Low Level and Lake Walks
Mountain Biking in the Lake District
Outdoor Adventures with Children – Lake District
Scrambles in the Lake District – North
Scrambles in the Lake District – South
The Cumbria Way
Trail and Fell Running in the Lake District
Walking the Lake District Fells:
  Borrowdale
  Buttermere
  Coniston
  Keswick
  Langdale
  Mardale and the Far East
  Patterdale
  Wasdale

DERBYSHIRE, PEAK DISTRICT AND MIDLANDS

Cycling in the Peak District
Dark Peak Walks
Scrambles in the Dark Peak
Walking in Derbyshire
Walking in the Peak District – White Peak East

For full information on all our guides, books and eBooks, visit our website:
www.cicerone.co.uk

CICERONE

Trust Cicerone to guide your next adventure, wherever it may be around the world...

Discover guides for hiking, mountain walking, backpacking, trekking, trail running, cycling and mountain biking, ski touring, climbing and scrambling in Britain, Europe and worldwide.

Connect with Cicerone online and find inspiration.

- buy books and ebooks
- articles, advice and trip reports
- podcasts and live events
- GPX files and updates
- regular newsletter

cicerone.co.uk